500
GOSPEL
SERMON OUTLINES

500
GOSPEL
SERMON OUTLINES

JOHN RITCHIE

KREGEL PUBLICATIONS
Grand Rapids, Michigan 49501

Library of Congress Cataloging-in-Publication Data

Ritchie, John 1853-1930.
    500 Gospel Sermon Outlines.

    Reprint. Originally published: Five Hundred Gospel Subjects. London: J. Ritchie, 1910.
    Includes index.
    1. Sermons — Outlines, syllabi, etc. I. Title.
II. Title: Five Hundred Gospel Subjects.
BV4223.R56   1987   251'.02   86-27760
ISBN 0-8254-3621-4

1 2 3 4 5 Printing/Year 91 90 89 88 87

Printed in the United States of America.

CONTENTS

Publisher's Preface 7

A Friendly Word to Preachers 9

Evangelistic Truths 17

Gospel Truths 59

Outlines on Bible Questions 96

Outlines on Types........................... 101

Outlines on Bible Texts 112

Outlines for Special Occasions 114

Funeral Outlines............................ 117

Blackboard Topics 119

Index 121

PUBLISHER'S PREFACE

"Preach the Word" was the admonition that Paul gave to the young preacher, Timothy (2 Tim. 4:2). What was so essential 2000 years ago is still necessary today. To "preach the Word" is to expound Scripture truths with clarity and conviction.

The *John Ritchie Sermon Outline* series has helped many to preach effectively since they were first published. Based on Scripture portions, these outlines bring out truths that change lives and minister to present needs. These aids are not intended to diminish a personal, prayerful study of the Bible. Rather, they will encourage it by giving insights to those who preach or teach God's truths.

These brief sermon outlines will enlighten, instruct and give direction to the believer as he walks the path marked out in the Word. They will also refresh and strengthen the inner man in his desire to better know God's word.

For the busy preacher or lay person who needs stimulating ideas for a dynamic preaching or teaching ministry, these sermon outlines will be most beneficial.

A FRIENDLY WORD
TO PREACHERS

A marked feature of the days of Gospel grace in which we live is, the large and ever-increasing number of earnest young preachers and soul-winners who are being raised up and sent forth to make known the glad tidings of salvation to sinners, in home and distant lands. The Lord increase their number and keep them right with Himself, so that they may be used of Him in the blessed and honorable work of gathering in the lost. No happier, no nobler work exists on earth, in which the energies of youth and the best and brightest years of life may be occupied for God, than in going forth with the Gospel message, heaven's last and costliest gift to men, seeking to win them to the Savior, to turn them from darkness to light, and from the power of Satan unto God. It is with the earnest desire to help along dear young fellow-laborers and soul-winners in this heavenly and holy service, and to encourage and cheer them in it, that we offer the following friendly words, not by commandment or with authority, but gathered from the Word and from daily experience and observation throughout a fairly wide field, extending along a course of over thirty years of Gospel service and continuous contact with others thus engaged.

First of all, we assume that all who go forth in the service of the Lord, making known His Gospel to others, have believed that Gospel themselves and have been definitely and Divinely converted: that they give unmistakable evidence that they are born of God, separated from the world, and so living and walking as to commend the message they declare. An unconverted Gospeller, or a worldly minded, flippant-living soul-winner, would be an anomaly indeed!

As a rule, true service for the Lord begins in a simple and unpretentious manner at home. "Go home to thy friends, and *tell them* how great things the Lord hath done for thee" (Mark 5:19), was the word to the newly saved Gadarene, and this is the way of the Lord always. If you have not testified to those in your home, your workshop, your street, your village, you need not expect to be led further afield. You must "qualify" in the lower class, the less public sphere, and "prove" yourself in the place where you are best known, before the Lord will entrust you in higher places, or fellow-believers have confidence in your ability to fill them. "The School of God" is the best and safest place for the young disciple, learning at the feet of Jesus, becoming acquainted with the Word of God, gathering the materials, and gaining the experiences he will require in days of public service.

All God's honored servants have had their periods of secret training alone with Himself before going forth to service: Moses in Horeb, David in the sheepfolds of Bethlehem, John in the deserts of Judea, and the great Soul-gatherer Himself, Jesus, the Son of God, in the solitudes of Nazareth. Yours may be the quiet home, the busy mart, the crowded city, the irksome post of duty in which your pride is humbled, your energies cribbed, your nature subdued, and your faith and patience tried — needed discipline for all who are to be set in places of temptation, responsibility and danger, in the service of God.

A *right condition* of soul is of the first importance in all who go forth with the Gospel, whatever the sphere may be, or whether the congregation consist of hundreds of intelligent, well-to-do hearers, or of half a dozen of the lapsed masses down an alley. The preacher must be right with God before he can have power with men. The vessel must be clean and empty — clean from sin and empty of self — in order to be filled with the power of God. The fisherman's eye is first turned to the sky, before he sets his hand to his boat or nets. See always that all is clear above, no cloud between your soul and God, nothing to hinder the Spirit of God from operating in and through you, before going forth to preach. It is well to always see God's face before you see the people: to have a season alone with God in heart-searching, self-judgment, prayer, and intercession, before going out in service. And if the service is long continued, this should be repeated again and again. No tool can constantly be used and still retain its edge: it must be taken again and again to the anvil or the grindstone, else cast aside as out of condition. Be much with God about your service: get your orders direct from Him; make it your aim to please Him first, and take little notice of either the flatteries or the frowns of men.

In regard to *the message* you deliver, seek it, get it from God. All God's Word is your armory, this Gospel is the same for one and all, yet the right word for that place, that people, and that time, must be given you by the Spirit of God if it is to be effectual. The whole Word of God is your textbook: the Gospel as set forth in type, history, parable, doctrine, text, and grouping, is all within your reach, and should be searched, studied, meditated on daily, not to be preached to others, but to feed, renew, edify, instruct, and refresh your own soul, and furnish you with all that you may require in the hour you are called upon to bear witness to or proclaim the Gospel. You need to take in fresh supplies daily if you are to give out fresh streams to others. The outflow can never exceed the inflow. Only as you make the Word of God your daily companion, and gather the manna fresh from its pages for your own soul's edification and strength, will you be able to bring out from your treasure "things new and old" (Matt. 15:32) for the blessing of others.

Whatever books you read, whatever teaching you hear, whatever "helps" you use or "subjects" you have suggested to you, let them guide you to the Word of God, never from it. Do not traffic in unfelt truths, or deal in other people's diggings: make the truth your own by study, meditation, and mastication. Steep the seed you are to sow in prayer, harrow it in by supplication when sown. Do not walk in borrowed plumes, adopting the phrases, imitating the styles, or trying to preach like somebody else. Be yourself: speak as before God in Christ; remember you have God and the devil always in your audience, and all Heaven looking on and listening every time you speak. Never prepare a cast-iron address, or commit to memory or manuscript a "speech" for delivery. Have the truth richly dwelling in you, its various aspects or divisions before you, then cast yourself upon the Spirit of God for guidance as to what to give out then and there.

Have confidence in the Gospel. It is the power of God unto salvation, the Divinely chosen instrument He is using for the conversion of sinners. It needs no embellishment, it requires no garnishing: it is "the Gospel of God," and it never fails in its object. The Holy Spirit has come to make it effectual. Count on His operations, leave room for His workings, have faith in His ability, lay yourself out to be His instrument. He is the Director of the work, the Controller of the servants (Acts 16:6, 7), and the Power by which the salvation of men is accomplished. All human arrangements must yield to Him, and in order to be free to go as and where He may lead (Acts 8:29), the servant of the Lord must be free from human fetters, under no church or committee control, free from the dominion of self-will and men-pleasing, in order to humbly, yet promptly, obey the Lord's calls and the Spirit's guidance.

The four R's of man's *ruin*, Christ's *redemption*, the Spirit's *regeneration*, and the hearer's *responsibility* should be clearly, fully, and constantly kept to the front, always making plentiful use of the words of Holy Scripture. God's own Word is more effectual than the clearest arguments, the most lucid reasonings, the simplest illustrations, and is the Word by which conviction is produced, the seed through which life is generated in the soul. Illustrations should be used carefully and sparingly; their use being only as the feather to the arrow. Incidents, stories, use only to elucidate, point, and press home the truth, never to amuse or raise a laugh. Avoid theological phrases; never use "slang"; do not make personal references to persons, places, or systems.

Preach Christ: exalt the Lamb of God, sound forth the fulness and freeness of God's salvation, the certainty of it to all who believe; the blood of Christ to cleanse, the power of Christ to deliver and to keep, with the eternal doom of all who despise or neglect it. Break up the fallow ground, plough deep, assail the conscience, bring your hearers face to face with God. Sin must be exposed, the sinner brought to see himself, own his guilt, justify God, and condemn himself, before he will either heed, hear, or believe the Gospel. False profession, light work, and Christless Christianity, are largely due to lack of the preaching that produces conviction, arouses the devil, and delivers sinners from his grasp. Depend upon it, if Satan's kingdom is in danger, he will roar, raise opposition, and vent his rage on the preacher and the converts. He did so to Christ and His apostles. He has continued the same in one form or another all along the line of battle. If you are personally assailed, leave your defense in the hands of God, and go on. He will guard your character.

Gift, grace, and *gumption* are all needed for public ministry, which all do not possess, and apart from which no one will long continue either to hold or have a people to hear him. Gift is a thing of measure: some have five talents, others ten. Care should be taken not to exceed the measure of gift or grace possessed. Some who can speak to a score in a cottage, are unfit to address a thousand in a hall: it would be wrong to try it. A man's gift makes room for him, and where the gift is, and grace to use it, it will sooner or later be recognized. Experience is gained by using what we have. A gift well and wisely used, develops and grows — according to the Word, "to him that hath shall be given," while one neglected and unused rusts away. Mistakes and failures ought to humble, but not discourage. Whatever helps to lowly thoughts of self and to more dependence upon God, is good.

It is god-like to encourage and pray for a young preacher, but devil-like to lavish fulsome flattery upon him, to puff him up with pride and self-importance. Many have been ruined by well-meaning but unwise adulation. "Hardness" is safer, and not likely to be awanting, if God's glory is the supreme object, and faithfulness to Christ the preacher's aim. If God uses your efforts, keep humble; if He uses others', rejoice. The Master uses the tool nearest to His hand and best fitted for His purpose. Study to present yourself as and where He may find you, if He sees fit to use you. If He does not, then search your ways, there will be a cause.

Open-air preaching reaches thousands who cannot be reached by any other means. The Master preached often in the open air: by the sea, on the hill, in the place of concourse. Paul evangelized by a riverside, in the marketplace, on Mars' Hill. If the people do not come to the Gospel, we must take the Gospel to them. Those who have the most ability are needed to preach the Word to the open-air crowd, whose attention has to be secured and held all the time: it is not to be regarded as a practicing ground for probationers and novices. Preach solidly, searchingly, solemnly, there; not random shot interspersed with song and story, but the Word in all its scope and fulness. Some will never hear the truth, unless they hear it there. Speak to be heard, not in a whisper, not in a roar. If possible, get the people inside after, to gather up results, deal with inquirers, and lead anxious ones to Christ.

Personal dealing should follow public preaching, and an opportunity given for seeking souls and those in difficulty to express their thoughts. Here is the true soul-winner's opportunity and here the sphere for many who never speak in public, true fellow-laborers and fellow-helpers in the Gospel all the same, whose praises are in all the churches. Never unduly press any to say they believe; never extort a confession of their faith. Seek from God the right text, the fitting word, the special presentation of Christ and the Gospel, to meet their special need. Lead them gently, and, as you bring Christ before them in the Gospel, bring them to God and Christ in prayer: lay hold on God for the sinner in faith as you lay hold on the sinner for God in earnest, loving effort. What a joy to see the mighty deliverance wrought, to witness the passage of a soul out of the darkness into light, to feel the first warm pulses of the new life, to be a sharer in the joy of Heaven over a newborn child of God, a fresh trophy of redeeming grace.

God bless all preachers of the Gospel of His grace, multiply their number, and give them abiding fruit in conversions. This is what the Gospel is preached for, and what its preachers should expect. According to their faith, so shall it be. "Blessed are ye that sow beside all waters" (Isa. 32:20). "He that winneth souls is wise" (Prov. 11:30). "And they that be wise shall shine as the brightness of the firmament; and they that turn many to righteousness as the stars for ever and ever" (Dan 12:3). The time is short, the world's dark night is coming. The Lord is at hand with His reward and crown for faithful service.

EVANGELISTIC TRUTHS

1   Three "Onlys"

Leaves Only (Matt. 21:19)—All man gives to God
Jesus Only (Matt. 17:8)—What God gives to Man
Believe Only (Luke 8:50)—God's way of salvation

> The *First* is man's empty *profession*
> The Second is God's priceless *possession*
> The Third is the soul's joyful *confession*

2   Three Great Questions

What have I done? (Jer. 8:6)—Careless Sinner
What must I do? (Acts 16:30)—Anxious Sinner
What shall I do? (Matt. 27:22)—Undecided Sinner

These tell the progress of a soul from indifference to anxiety, then to decision for, or against, Christ.

3   Three Deaths

Dead *in* Sin (Eph. 2:1)—The Sinner
Dead *for* Sin (1 Cor. 15:3)—The Savior
Dead *to* Sin (Rom. 6:2)—The Saint

> The *First* is the natural condition of all men
> The *Second* is the Gospel of God for all men
> The *Third* is the Result to those that believe

4   Peace

Peace Procured (Col. 1:20)—At the Cross
Peace Preached (Eph. 2:17)—In the Gospel
Peace Possessed (Rom. 5:1)—By the Believer

5   Four Suppers

Supper of *grace* (Luke 14:16)—In the Gospel
Supper of *communion* (1 Cor. 11:20)—In the Church
Supper of *glory* (Rev. 19:9)—In the Glory
Supper of *judgment* (Rev. 19:17)—On the Earth

All who accept the invitation to the first, are thereby fitted to be sharers in the second, and sure to be at the third. All who despise the first, are uninvited to the second, prohibited from the third, but will be compelled to the fourth.

6   Three "Beholdings" of Christ

Beholding the *Dying* One (John 1:29)—Salvation
Beholding *Risen* One (2 Cor. 3:18)—Transformation
Beholding *Coming* One (1 John 3:2)—Glorification

7   Three Fundamental Truths

Redemption by *Blood* (1 Peter 1:19)—Work of Son
Resurrection by *Power* (1 Peter 1:21)—Work of Father
Regeneration through the *Word* (1 Peter 1:23)—Work of
the Spirit

These great fundamental truths should be clearly set forth in every Gospel address.

8   The Water of Life

Its Source—In God (Jer. 2:13; Ps. 36:9)
Its Flow—From Christ (John 4:14; Rev. 22:1)
Its Channels—Through Believers (John 7:38, 39)
Its Receivers—The Thirsty (Isa. 55:1; Rev. 21:6)

9   Three Solemn Facts
(Job 36:18)

Coming Wrath, with Rom. 2:5; Rev. 6:17
Sudden Death, with Prov. 29:1; Job 21:13
Eternal Punishment, with 2 Thess. 1:9; Matt. 25:46

10   Salvation in Four Aspects

The Salvation of God (Acts 28:28)

A Great Salvation (Heb. 2:3)

A Common Salvation (Jude 3)

An Eternal Salvation (Heb. 5:9)

    It is *of* God, *for* man, *from* sin and hell, *unto* eternal glory (2 Tim. 2:10).

11   Grace

Its Source—God (1 Peter 5:10; Rom. 5:15)

Its Manifestation—In Christ (John 1:14, 17; 2 Cor. 8:9)

Its Character—Rich (Eph. 1:7; Abundant (1 Tim. 1:14)

Its Subjects—Sinners (1 Tim. 1:14, 17; 1 Cor. 15:10)

Its Operations—Justifies (Rom. 3:24); Saves (Eph. 2:5)

12   "No Mores"

No more Offering for Sins (Heb. 10:18, with 9:26)

No more Remembrance of Sins (Heb. 10:17, with Isa. 44:22)

No more Conscience of Sins (Heb. 10:2, with 10:22)

No more Continuance in Sin (John 5:14, with Rom. 6:1)

13   God's "Abundant" Things

Abundant Mercy (1 Peter 1:3)—For the Lost

Abundant Grace (1 Tim. 1:14)—For the Needy

Abundant Pardon (Isa. 55:7)—For the Guilty

Abundant Life (John 10:10)—For the Dead

Abundant Power (Eph. 3:20)—For the Weak

Abundant Peace (Ps. 37:11)—For the Troubled

Abundant Joy (Phil. 1:26)—For the Sad

14   How God Forgives Sinners

Frankly (Luke 7:42, with Eph. 1:7)

Freely (Eph. 4:32, with Acts 13:38, 39)

Fully (Col. 2:13, with Heb. 10:17)

15   Four Gospel "Mys"

My Soul (Isa. 38:17)—A Valuable Possession
My Sins (Isa. 38:17)—A Weighty Burden
My Savior (Luke 1:47)—A Great Deliverer
My Salvation (Isa. 12:2)—A Joyful Confession

   Awakened to own the value of the first, to feel the burden of the second, the sinner is led to the third, and soon knows and rejoices in the fourth.

16   The Lord Jesus

In Isaiah 53

The Tender Plant (v. 2)—In Youth
The Man of Sorrows (v. 3)—In Service
The Sinbearer (v. 6)—On the Cross
The Substitute (v. 8)—In Death
The Justifier (v. 11)—In Resurrection

17   Out of the Pit Into the Service

(Psalm 40:1-3)

State by Nature (v. 2)—In the pit and the clay
Salvation by Grace (v. 2)—Brought up and out of both
Standing in Christ (v. 2)—Set upon a Rock
Stability for Christ (v. 2)—Established my goings
Song of Thanksgiving (v. 3)—Put new song in mouth
Saintly Testimony (v. 3)—Many shall see
Service & Soulwinning (v. 3)—And trust in the Lord

18   Reserved and Kept

Heaven reserved for Saints (1 Peter 1:5)
Saints kept for Heaven (1 Peter 1:5)
Hell reserved for Sinners (2 Peter 2:17)
Sinners reserved for Hell (2 Peter 2:9)

   The contrast here is striking and solemn. The same power that saves and keeps the believing sinner, reserves the unjust for judgment.

19   The Great White Throne
(Revelation 20:11-15)

The Throne of Judgment, v. 2 (with Ps. 9:7; Eccl. 11:9)
The Appointed Judge, v. 2 (with Acts 17:31; John 5:22)
The Culprits, v. 12 (with John 5:27-30; Rom. 2:12)
The Opened Books, v. 13 (with Eccl. 12:14; John 12:48)
The Final Sentence, v. 13 (with Eccl. 8:2; 2 Peter 2:9)
The Eternal Doom, v. 15 (with Mark 9:43-46; 16:16)

20   Three Blessings, in John 10:9
True of all who enter through Christ, the Door

Salvation—*"Shall be saved"* (see also Eph. 2:8)
Liberty—*"Go in and out"* (see also Heb. 10:22; 13:13)
Food—*"And find pasture"* (see also Ps. 23:2)

21   The Two Roads

Two Gates (Matt. 7:13)—The Wide and the Strait
Two Roads (Matt. 7:14)—The Broad and the Narrow
Two Classes (Matt. 7:14)—The Many and the Few
Two Destinies (Matt. 7:14)—Destruction and Life
No middle path, no third class, no intermediate destiny

22   Far Off and Nigh

Far off—By Nature (Eph. 2:12). By Practice (Isa. 59:2)
Nigh—By Blood (Eph. 2:13). By Faith (Heb. 10:22)

23   A Threefold Cord of Love

God's Love to the *World* (John 3:16)—Universal
Christ's Love for the Church (Eph. 5:25)—Special
The *Father's Love* to the *Family* (1 John 3:1)—Parental

24   Three "Unspeakable" Things

God's Unspeakable Gift (2 Cor. 9:15)
The Believer's Unspeakable Joy (1 Peter 1:8)
Heaven's Unspeakable Words (2 Cor. 12:4)

> To receive the *gift*, is the way to experience the *joy*, and to reach *Heaven*

25   Divine Forgiveness

The Divine Author—God (Eph. 4:32)
The Procuring Cause—The Blood of Christ (Eph. 1:7)
The Obtaining Means—Faith (Acts 13:39)
The Source of Assurance—God's Word (Col. 2:13)
The Sure Result—Blessedness (Rom. 4:7)

26   Divine Certainties

Death of the Sinner (1 Kings 2:37, with Heb. 9:27)
Penury of the Sinner (1 Tim. 6:7, with Job 21:13)
Judgment of the Sinner (Heb. 10:27, with Rom. 2:2)
Gospel for the Sinner (Luke 1:4, with Gal. 1:11)
Salvation of the Sinner (Rom. 10:9, with Isa. 12:2)

27   Four Views of Christ's Work

(Deuteronomy 32:10)

He Found Him, Conversion—Christ, the Savior
He Led Him, Obedience—Christ, the Shepherd
He Instructed Him, Discipleship—Christ, the Teacher
He Kept Him, Preservation—Christ, the Preserver

28   Four Present Blessings

The Possession of All Believers

Forgiveness of Sins (Acts 10:43, with Acts 13:38, 39)
Eternal Life (John 20:31, with John 6:47; 5:24)
Salvation (Acts 16:31, with Rom. 10:9)
Joy and Peace (Rom. 15:13, with Rom. 5:1-3)

29   Three Classes on Mars' Hill

(Acts 17)

Mockers (v. 32)—"Some *mocked*"
Procrastinators (v. 32)—"We will hear thee *again*"
Believers (v. 34)—"Certain men . . . *believed*"

30   Three Reigns

(Romans 5:17-21)

Death Reigned (v. 17)—From Adam till Christ
Grace Reigns (v. 21)—From the Cross to the Lord's Coming
Reign in Life (v. 17)—From Resurrection and Forever

31   Four Straight Questions

To One Fleeing From the Presence of God
(Jonah 1)

What meanest thou? (v. 6)—Answer, Eccl. 9:3
What is thine occupation? (v. 8)—Answer, John 8:34
Whence comest thou? (v. 8)—Answer, Rom. 5:12
Of what people art thou? (v. 8)—Answer, Eph. 2:17

32   Some Bible Trees

Adam hiding *behind* a tree (Gen. 3:8)—Fallen Sinner
Zacchaeus *up* a tree (Luke 19:4)—Religious Sinner
Nathanael *under* a tree (John 1:48)—Convicted One
Jesus *on* a tree (Acts 10:39)—The Dying Savior

33   The Grace of God

(Titus 2:11-14)

The *Salvation* it brings us (v. 11)
The *Lessons* it teaches us (v. 12)
The *Hope* it sets before us (v. 13)

Salvation comes first, by grace through faith
Instruction comes next, in grace, unto godly living
Hope, awaits the consummation of grace in glory

34   The Triune God

(Luke 15)

The Shepherd seeking the Sheep (v. 4-7)—The Work of Christ

The Woman finding the Silver (v. 8-18)—The Work of the Spirit

The Father welcoming the Prodigal (v. 11-32)—The Work of the Father

35   Five Looks of Jesus

Look of Compassion (Matt. 9:36)—On the Perishing

Look of Desire (Mark 5:32)—On the Healed One

Look of Complacency (Mark 3:34)—On His Own

Look of Anger (Mark 3:5)—On the hardened sinner

Look of Pity (Luke 22:61)—On a Backslider

36   Christ Gave Himself

For *all* (1 Tim. 2:6)—The Widest Circle

For *many* (Mark 10:45)—The Believing Circle

For the *church* (Eph. 5:25)—The Elect Circle

For *me* (Gal 2:20)—The Personal Circle

There is a general and a special view of the work of the Cross. Both are true, but they should never be confounded.

37   Fourfold View of the Sinner

(Luke 15)

The Wandering Sheep (v. 4)—The Sinner Straying

The Lost Coin (v. 8)—Sinner Dead and Helpless

The Returning Son (v. 18)—The Sinner Repentant

The Self-righteous Son (v. 28)—Sinner despising grace

38   Three "Musts"

(John 3)

Ye must be born again (v. 7)—The sinner's "must"

The Son must be lifted up (v. 14)—Savior's "must"

I must decrease (v. 30)—The Servant's "must"

39   Three Comprehensive Words

Whosoever will, may take (Rev. 22:17)—The Sinner's Title
Whatsoever ye ask (John 14:13)—The Believer's Warrant
Whithersoever He goeth (Rev. 14:4)—The Disciple's Path

40   Earth, Heaven, Hell

(Luke 14, 15, 16)

The Gospel Feast—Sinners invited; receivers and neglecters described (Luke 14:15-24)—Earth

The Prodigal's Return—Reception and Restoration (Luke 15:21-24)—Heaven

The Rich Man's Life, Death, Burial, and Doom (Luke 16:19-26)—Hell

41   Five Yokes

The Yoke of Sin (Deut. 28:48; Prov. 5:22)—The Sinner's Slavery

The Yoke of Bondage (Gal. 5:1; Acts 15:10)—The Sinner's Religion

The Yoke of Christ (Lam. 1:14; Isa. 53:6)—The Sin-bearer's Burden

The Yoke of Obedience (Matt. 11:29, 30)—The Saint's Submission

The Yoke of Service (Phil. 4:3; 1 Tim. 6:1)—The Servant's Fellowship

42   Four "Cannots"

The natural man cannot please God (Rom. 8:8)
Corrupt tree cannot bear good fruit (Matt. 7:18)
Unregenerate cannot see the Kingdom (John 3:3)
The damned cannot pass from Hell (Luke 16:26)

43   Threefold Salvation

Present Salvation (Acts 16:30, 31; Eph. 2:8)
Progressive Salvation (Heb. 7:25; Phil. 2:12)
Prospective Salvation (Rom. 13:11; Heb. 9:28)

44   Three Salvation Truths
(Hebrews 10)

The Will of God (Heb. 10:7)—Source of Salvation
The Work of Christ (Heb. 10:10)—Cause of Salvation
Witness of the Spirit (Heb. 10:15)—Seal of Salvation

45   Four "Alls"

All gone astray (Isa. 53:6)—Ruin of all
Iniquity of *All* laid on Christ (Isa. 53:6)—Ransom for all
All that believe (Acts 13:39)—Forgiveness for all
From *All* things (Acts 13:39)—Justified from all

Enter in by the first "all," travel through the second and third, and come out at the last.

46   Three Appointments

Death (Heb. 9:27)—The Result of Sin
Judgment (Acts 17:31)—The Punishment of Sin
Salvation (1 Thess. 5:9)—Deliverance from Sin

47   Things Poured Out

Water poured out in *Confession* (1 Sam. 7:6; 2 Sam. 14:14)
Blood poured out in *Atonement* (Lev. 4:7; John 19:34)
Oil poured out in *Grace* (2 Kings 4:4; Acts 10:45)
Wrath poured out in *Judgment* (Rev. 19:10; Hos. 5:10)

48   Threefold Crucifixion

Christ crucified *for* me (Gal. 3:1, with Luke 23:33)
The Flesh crucified *in* me (Gal. 5:24, with Rom. 6:6)
The World crucified *to* me (Gal. 6:14, with Col. 2:20)

49   **Five Cups**

Cup of Judgment (Ps. 11:6)—The Sinner's Cup
Cup of Suffering (Matt. 26:39)—The Savior's Cup
Cup of Salvation (Ps. 116:13)—The Gospel Cup
Cup of Blessing (Ps. 23:5)—The Believer's Cup
Cup of Wrath (Rev. 19:10)—Christ-Rejecter's Cup

50   Fourfold Description of Man
(Romans 5)

"Without strength" (v. 6)
"Ungodly" (v. 6)
"Sinners" (v. 8)
"Enemies" (v. 9)

The death of Christ meets this fourfold need. There is no other remedy.

51   Look, Learn, Live

Look unto Me (Isa. 45:22)—Salvation
Learn of Me (Matt. 11:29)—Discipleship
Live by Me (John 6:57)—Life of Faith

52   Three Doors
(John 10)

The Door of the Shepherd (v. 1)—By which the Shepherd
    enters
The Door of the Sheep (v. 7)—Through which the Sheep are
    led out
The Door of Salvation (v. 9)—To enter for Salvation and
    Liberty

1. The Door of the Jewish fold, through which the True Shepherd
entered.
2. Himself the Door, through whom the sheep were led to enjoy greater
privileges.
3. The Door of Salvation, through which "any man" may now enter.

53   The Hand of the Lord

In Salvation (Acts 11:21)
In Protection (John 10:28)
In Judgment (Acts 13:11)

54   Three Divine Openings

Opened Heart (Acts 16:14)—To receive Christ
Opened Scriptures (Luke 24:32)—Reveal Christ
Opened Understanding (Luke 24:45)—Learn Christ

55   The Truth of God

The truth declared (Col. 1:6)—Preacher's Business
The truth believed (2 Thess. 2:13)—Hearer's Faith
The truth obeyed (1 Peter 1:22)—The Believer's Duty
The truth rejected (2 Thess. 2:10)—Unbeliever's Sin
The truth resisted (2 Tim. 2:8)—Opposer's Work
The truth changed (Rom. 1:25)—The Devil's Wile
The truth avenged (2 Thess. 2:12)—Rejecter's Doom

56   His Name

Remission in His Name (Acts 10:43)—Not by prayers
Life through His Name (John 20:31)—Not by works
Salvation in His Name (Acts 4:12)—In no other

57   First and Last Words of Jesus

"I must be about My Father's business" (Luke 2:49)
"It is finished" (John 19:30)

   The first uttered in the Temple; the last on the Cross

58   Faith and Works

Justified by Faith (Rom. 3:28)—Before God
Justified by Works (James 2:21-24)—Before men

59   **What the Word Does**

Life imparted by the Word (1 Peter 1:23)—Receive it
Life nourished by the Word (1 Peter 2:2)—Feed on it
Ways cleansed by the Word (Ps. 119:9)—Use it
Path enlightened by the Word (Ps. 119:105)—Walk in it

60   **Four Thrones**

Throne of Mercy (Exod. 25:17-22)—The Meeting place
    between God and Man
Throne of Grace (Heb. 4:16)—The Daily Resource of Saints
Throne of Glory (Rev. 4:3, 4)—The Destiny of the Redeemed
Throne of Judgment (Rev. 20:11)—The Retribution of the
    Lost

The first, is the propitiatory (Rom. 3:25), where the sinner meets God in mercy

The second, the throne of grace, where the saint in need draws near
The third, the throne in resurrection glory, to which the redeemed are to be brought

The fourth, the sphere or place of righteous judgment, at which the dead in sin will appear

61   **The Hands of Christ**

Pierced for our sin (Ps. 22:16)—The Dying One
Shown for our peace (John 20:20)—The Risen One
Uplifted for blessing (Luke 24:50)—Ascending One
Opened for our supply (Ps. 145:16)—Glorified One

62   **Two Great Works**

The Work of Christ *for* us (John 17:4)—Perfect and
    Complete
The Work of the Spirit *in* us (Phil. 1:6)—Progressive and
    Prospective

63 The Sinner's Destitution

The Unconverted are described as being—

Without God (Eph. 2:12)
Without Christ (Eph. 2:12)
Without Hope (Eph. 2:12)
Without Strength (Rom. 5:6)
Without Excuse (Rom. 1:20)

These are all true, always, of every unregenerate man

64 Life in the Spirit

Imparted by the Spirit (John 3:5)—Regeneration
Springing up in the Spirit (John 4:14)—Worship, Godward
Outflowing through the Spirit (John 7:38)—Testimony, Manward

65 Four Handwritings

On Tables of Stone (Exod. 34:1)—Law
On the Plaster of the Wall (Dan. 5:5)—Judgment
On the Cross (Matt. 27:37)—Atonement
On the Heart (2 Cor. 3:2)—Grace

1. The Sinner tested and found wanting
3. The Sinner judged for sin and impiety
3. The Savior working out Redemption
4. The Believer manifesting the result of Regeneration

66 Cleansing

Cleansing by Blood (Heb. 9:14, 22)—Result of Cross
Cleansing by Water (John 13:1-10)—Daily use of Word

The first is never repeated; in virtue of it the believing sinner is regarded as abidingly clean before God. The second is never to be neglected, because by it the believer is kept clean in his ways before men.

67   Four Foundation Facts

Ruin by Adam's Fall (Rom. 5:12-14)—Our Ruin
Redemption by Blood (Heb. 9:11, 12)—God's remedy
Regeneration by the Spirit (John 3:5)—Our Need
Reception by faith (Acts 16:31)—Our responsibility

68   Seven Eternal Things

Eternal God (Deut. 33:27)—The Source of all
Eternal Redemption (Heb. 9:12)—The Cause of all
Eternal Salvation (Heb. 5:9)—God's Greatest Work
Eternal Life (Rom. 6:23)—God's Richest Gift
Eternal Inheritance (Heb. 9:15)—Saint's possession
Eternal Glory (1 Peter 5:10)—The Believer's Hope
Eternal Fire (Jude 7)—The Sinner's Doom

If the one is eternal, enduring for ever, so are the others. To limit one is to weaken all.

69   Acceptance

Accepted *for* Him (Lev. 1:4)—Substitution
Accepted *in* the Beloved (Eph. 1:6)—Standing
Accepted *of* Him (2 Cor. 5:9)—Service

70   Faith in Four Aspects

Justified by faith (Rom. 5:1)—The Believer's Place
Standing by faith (2 Cor. 1:24)—Believer's Foothold
Living by faith (Gal. 2:20)—Believer's Sustenance
Walking by faith (2 Cor. 5:7)—Believer's Progress

71   Unto Himself

Reconciled unto Himself (Col. 1:20)—By the Cross
Set apart for Himself (Ps. 3:3)—By the Spirit
Purified unto Himself (Titus 2:14)—By the Truth
Subdued unto Himself (Phil. 3:21)—By His Power
Presented to Himself (Eph. 5:27)—In the Glory

72 God and His People

God *for* us (Rom. 8:31)—Our Justifier
God *with* us (Heb. 13:5)—Our Defender
God *in* us (2 Cor. 6:16)—Our Indweller

73 Threefold Glory of Christ

A Worm (Ps. 22:6)—Suffering in Weakness
A Shepherd (Ps. 23:1)—Guiding in Faithfulness
A King (Ps. 24:7)—Reigning in Righteousness

74 Three Words

"Fear not" (Isa. 43:1)—The Word of Pardon
"Fret not" (Ps. 37:1)—The Word of Peace
"Faint not" (2 Cor. 4:16)—The Word of Power

75 What God Is

(Psalm 32)

God our Justifier (v. 1)—The Sinner's Salvatin
God our Hiding-place (v. 7)—The Saint's Security
God our Guide (v. 8)—The Pilgrim's Safeguard

76 Witnesses to Christ

The Father's Testimony (Matt. 3:17)—Divine
The Scriptures' Testimony (John 5:39)—Inspired
The Believer's Testimony (Song of Sol. 5:16)—Experimental
The World's Testimony (John 7:46)—Human
The Demons' Testimony (Luke 8:28)—Infernal

77 Three Stages in Work of Grace

Saved by Grace (Eph. 2:8)—Power in Salvation
Standing in Grace (Rom. 5:2)—Position of Saved
Growing in Grace (2 Peter 3:18)—Progress of Saved

78   Eyes Opened

To their sin and shame (Gen. 3:7)—Conviction
To Christ and Salvation (Acts 26:18)—Conversion
In Hell, amid torment (Luke 16:23)—Christ-rejection

79   Things That Are Short

Time is short (1 Cor. 7:29)
Life is short (Ps. 39:5)
The Sinner's Joy is short (Job 20:5)
The Saint's affliction is short (2 Cor. 4:17)

80   Trumpets

Of Danger (Ezek. 33:3)—Giving Warning
Of Redemption (Lev. 25:8-10)—Giving Liberty
Of Resurrection (1 Cor. 15:51)—Raising the Dead
Of Judgment (Rev. 9:14)—Announcing Wrath

81   Four Crowns

Of Thorns (Matt. 27:29)—The Savior's Crown
Of Gold (Rev. 4:4)—The Saint's Crown
Of Rejoicing (1 Thess. 2:19)—The Servant's Crown
Of Glory (1 Peter 5:4)—The Shepherd's Crown

The Savior's was the fruit of the curse; the saint's is the fruit of the Cross; the servant's and the shepherd's are the Master's rewards for faithful service.

82   Nothings

We can do nothing (John 15:5)—Helpless
We have nothing (1 Tim. 6:7)—Beggars
We know nothing (1 Cor. 8:2)—Ignorant
We are good for nothing (Matt. 5:13)—Useless
We are nothing (Gal. 6:3)—Ciphers

This knowledge is not taught in the world's schools

83   Vessels

Vessels of Wrath (Rom. 9:22)—For Destruction
Vessels of Mercy (Rom. 9:23)—For Glory
Vessels unto Honor (2 Tim. 2:21)—For Service

> Sin fits for hell; God's mercy and Christ's work fit for glory; separation from evil makes fit for service to God

84   The Joy of God

In the Salvation of the Lost (Luke 15:28)
In the Obedience of the Saved (3 John 4)
In the Glorification of His Own (Jude 24)

85   The Sinner's Hope

The Hope of the Unjust (Prov. 11:7)
The Hope of the Hypocrite (Job 8:13)
A Lost Hope (Ezek. 37:11)

86   The Believer's Hope

Christ in you the Hope of Glory (Col. 1:27)
The Hope laid up in Heaven (Col. 1:5)
A Living Hope (1 Peter 1:3)
A Purifying Hope (1 John 3:3)
A Sure Hope (Heb. 6:19)

87   Three "Withouts"

Without Holiness (Heb.12:14)—No seeing of God
Without Blood (Heb. 9:22)—God cannot Justify
Without Faith (Heb. 11:6)—No pleasing of God

88   Fools

The Infidel Fool (Ps. 14:1)—Wise in his conceit
The Worldly Fool (Luke 12:20)—Wise only for time
The Self-righteous Fool (Prov. 28:6)—Wise in his ignorance
The Christian Fool (1 Cor. 4:10)—Wise for Eternity

89   Three Present Blessings

Justified by Christ (Gal. 2:17)—Our Righteousness
Sanctified to Christ (Heb. 13:12)—Our Holiness
Accepted in Christ (Eph. 1:6)—Our Standing

90   "Fear Not"

Spoken by the Lord in varied circumstances

To the Shepherds (Luke 2:10)—In the Fields
To the new Convert (Luke 5:10)—On the Seashore
To the anxious Father (Luke 8:50)—By a Deathbed
To the earnest Servant (Acts 27:34)—In a Storm
To the exiled Disciple (Rev. 1:17)—In Patmos

The order of these is—Gospel, confidence, assurance, encouragement, strength

91   Threefold Deliverance

(2 Corinthians 1:10)

Who *hath* delivered (Ps. 86:13; 1 Thess. 1:10)—Past
Who *doth* deliver (2 Peter 2:9; 2 Tim. 4:18)—Present
Who *shall* deliver (Rom. 7:24; 8:21)—Future

The first effected by the Death of Christ
The second is wrought by the Risen Christ
The third will be at the Coming of Christ

92   Individual Conversations

In John's Gospel

Nathanael, a guileless Israelite (John 1:47)
Nicodemus, a learned Pharisee (John 3:1)
Woman of Samaria, an alien sinner (John 4)
Impotent Man, a helpless cripple (John 5:5)
Condemned Woman, an abandoned sinner (John 8:10)
Blind Man, a miracle of power (John 9:35)

Each different, yet all came to and conversed with the same Savior; all were saved with the common salvation

93   Three Stages in the Soul's Progress

Beholding, hearing, following (John 1:9)—Conversion
Confessing, desiring, abiding (John 1:38)—Communion
Communing, testifying (John 1:40, 41)—Witness-bearing

94   Unfruitful Seed

In Matthew 13

The Wayside Hearer (v. 4)—The Indifferent—Satan the Cause

The Stony Ground (v. 5)—The Professor—The Flesh—No Life

The Thorny Ground (v. 7)—The Worldling—Its Cares and Pleasures

Three classes of Gospel hearers, present wherever Christ is preached

95   The Man, Christ Jesus

(A Sevenfold Testimony to the Lord Jesus)

Never man spake like this Man (John 7:46)—The Officers
This Man receiveth sinners (Luke 15:2)—The Pharisees
This Man hath done nothing amiss (Luke 23:41)—The Robber
This Man was the Son of God (Mark 15:39)—The Centurion
Not this Man, but Barabbas (John 18:40)—People
This Man was counted worthy (Heb. 3:3)—God, the Father
Through this Man is forgiveness (Acts 13:38)—Paul

96   Gospel A B C

All have sinned (Rom. 3:23)
Be sure your sin will find you out (Num. 32:23)
Christ died for our sins (1 Cor. 15:3)
Dost thou believe on the Son of God? (John 9:35)

97   Four Seals

Man's Sins Sealed (Job 14:17)—For Judgment
The Savior Sealed (John 6:37)—For Sacrifice
The Believer's Seal (John 3:33)—Seal of Faith
God's Seal (Eph. 1:13)—Seal of the Spirit

Sins recorded and sealed await the Judgment. The Seal on the Son of God bears witness to His fitness as Sacrifice and Savior. The believer sets to His seal that God is true when he receives His record, and God sets His seal upon him, making and claiming him as His own.

98   Sevenfold Virtue of the Blood

It procures Redemption (Eph. 1:6)—For the Slave
It secures Justification (Rom. 5:9)—For the Guilty
It ensures Cleansing (1 John 1:7)—For the Unclean
It assures Peace (Col. 1:20)—For the Troubled
It effects Sanctification (Heb. 13:12)—For the Unholy
It gives Nearness (Eph. 2:13)—For the Alien
It brings Victory (Rev. 12:11)—For the Accused

99   Four "One Things"

One thing thou lackest (Mark 10:21)—Salvation
One thing I know (John 9:25)—Assurance
One thing is needful (Luke 10:42)—Communion
One thing I do (Phil. 3:13)—Devotion

100   Three Representative Men
(Hebrews 11:4-6)

Abel came *to* God (v. 4, with Gen. 3)
Enoch walked *with* God (v. 5, with Gen. 5)
Noah wrought *for* God (v. 6, with Gen. 6)

This is the Divine order. Man as a sinner must first come to God through sacrifice, by faith, before he can walk with God as a friend, or work for God as a servant.

101   Seven "I Ams"

In John's Gospel

I am the *Door* (10:9)—To enter by
I am the *Way* (14:6)—To walk in
I am the *Bread* (6:47)—To feed upon
I am the *Shepherd* (10:11)—To guide
I am the *Light* (8:12)—To follow
I am the *True Vine* (15:1)—To abide in
I am the *Resurrection* (6:25)—To wait for

102   What Christ Is Able to Do

He is able to *save* (Heb. 7:25)
He is able to *deliver* (Dan. 3:17)
He is able to *make stand* (Rom. 14:4)
He is able to *keep* (Jude 24)
He is able to *succor* (Heb. 2:18)

103 Seven Things God Says Are "Ready"

The Sinner is "ready to perish" (Deut. 26:3)
God is "ready to pardon" (Neh. 9:17)
Jesus is "ready to save" (Isa. 38:20)
The Saint is "ready to every good work" (Titus 3:1)
The Servant is "ready to preach" (Rom. 1:15)
The Glory is "ready to be revealed" (1 Peter 1:5)
The Lord is "ready to judge" (1 Peter 4:5)

104   The Bow and the Cloud

The Bow in the Cloud (Gen. 9:13)—Grace
The Cloud without a Bow (Luke 21:27)—Judgment
The Bow without a Cloud (Rev. 4:3)—Glory

The First is the symbol of God's present attitude toward man
The Second is the symbol of what God will do hereafter
The Third is the symbol of the Eternal Glory

105   Eternal Life in Three Aspects

Eternal Life in *Promise* (Titus 1:2)—Past
Eternal Life in *Possession* (1 John 5:13)—Present
Eternal Life in *Prospect* (Jude 21)—Future

God's promise of the past has now become His gift (Rom. 6:23), and whoever accepts it as such, has it in him as a present possession (1 John 5:9), while he waits for its full fruition in glory.

106   Three Calls From Christ

The *Savior's* Call—"Come unto Me" (Matt. 11:28)
The *Master's* Call—"Learn of Me" (Matt. 11:29)
The *Shepherd's* Call—"Follow Me" (John 21:19)

The religious man tries to learn and follow before he really comes to Christ. Conversion must ever precede Discipleship.

107   The Salvation of God

The Author of Salvation (Heb. 5:9)—The Lord Jesus
The Way of Salvation (Acts 16:17)—Through Faith
Knowledge of Salvation (Luke 1:77)—By the Word
The Joy of Salvation (Ps. 51:12)—In the Believer
The Day of Salvation (2 Cor. 6:2)—Now

Salvation is of the Lord—for all, but only possessed by those who believe. The knowledge of it comes by believing the Word, and the joy of it follows. The latter may be lost; it will be if, through sin, the Spirit is grieved and communion is broken. By confession, both are restored.

108   Forgiveness of Sins

Provided by Grace (Eph. 1:7)—God, the Provider
Procured by Blood (Col. 1:13)—Christ, the Cause
Proclaimed in Gospel (Acts 13:38)—In the Spirit
Possessed by Believers (1 John 2:12)—Through Faith

109   Threefold Judgment

The Savior's (Isa. 53:5, with John 5:54)—Past
The Saint's (1 Peter 1:17; 1 Cor. 11:32)—Present
The Sinner's (John 5:28, 29; Rev. 20:11)—Future

Judgment for sin the Savior bore; into it the believer does not come. If he err or sin, he should judge himself; if he fail in this, God will. The unbeliever's judgment is to come.

110   Four Steps in a Sinner's History
(Isaiah 6:1-9)

Convicted of sin (v. 5)—The Action of the Light
Cleansed from sin (v. 7)—The Result of Sacrifice
Consecrated to God (v. 8)—Effect of Conversion
Commissioned by God (v. 9)—The Call to Service

111   Precious Things

Precious Souls (Ps. 49:8)—Subject of Redemption
Precious Blood (1 Peter 1:19)—Redemption Price
Precious Christ (1 Peter 2:7)—The Great Redeemer
Precious Faith (2 Peter 1:1)—Appropriating Hand
Precious Promises (2 Peter 1:4)—Portion of the Saint

112   Tears

The Savior's Tears (Luke 19:41)—Compassion
Saved Sinners's Tears (Luke 7:38, 44)—Contrition
Soul-winner's Tears (Acts 20:19, 31)—Earnestness
The Backslider's Tears (Luke 8:62)—Sorrow
The Lost Sinner's Tears (Heb. 12:7)—Remorse

113   A Question and Its Answer

What shall the end be of them that obey not the Gospel?
    (1 Peter 4:17)
Answer—Phil. 3:19; 2 Thess. 1:8, 9

114 Universal Depravity

All gone astray (Isa. 53:6)—The Indictment
All have sined (Rom. 3:23)—The Verdict
Death come upon all (Rom. 5:12)—The Result
Judgment awaiting all (Heb. 9:27)—The Prospect

115 Three Classes in Hell

Neglecters of salvation (Heb. 2:3)—Too busy to take
Rejecters of salvation (John 12:48)—Too proud to need
Despisers of salvation (Acts 13:41)—Too wise to heed

116 Two Divine Realities

"Every whit made *clean*" (John 13:10)
"Every whit made *whole*" (John 7:23)

The Precious Blood of Christ makes clean
The Mighty Power of Christ makes whole

117 A Revival at Thessalonica

(The Preacher, the Preaching, the Power)

Christ, the Preacher's *Theme* (Acts 17:3)
The Scriptures, the Preacher's *Book* (Acts 17:2)
The Holy Spirit, the Preacher's *Power* (1 Thess. 1:5)
Holy, the Preacher's *Character* (1 Thess. 2:10)

These are four essentials to a genuine Revival

118 God and the Sinner

(His Attitude in Five Respects regarding Salvation)

Permitted—Whosoever will, let him take (Rev. 22:17)
Invited—Come, for all things are ready (Luke 14:17)
Entreated—God did beseech by us (2 Cor. 2:10)
Commanded—His commandment...believe (1 John 3:23)
Compelled—Compel them to come in (Luke 14:23)

119 A Threefold Cord of Salvation

Chosen by God the Father (Eph. 1:4)—In the Past
Redeemed by God the Son (Eph. 1:7)—At the Cross
Sealed by God the Spirit (Eph. 1:13)—On Believing

120 Two Divine Facts

It is Finished (John 19:30)—Perfect Work of Christ
It is Written (Matt. 4:4)—Eternal Word of God

> The Work of Christ makes the believing sinner *safe*
> The Word of God makes the believing sinner *sure*

121 Four Contrasts

(Luke 16:19-23)

Two Men (vv. 19, 20)—In Nature and in Grace
Two Lives (vv. 19-21)—Christian and Christless
Two Deaths (v. 22)—In Faith, or in Sin
Two Destinies (vv. 22, 23)—Heaven and Hell

> No difference (Rom. 3:23) to begin with, the two ways part at the Cross

122 Four Jehovah Titles

Jehovah-Jireh, "The Lord will provide" (Gen. 22:14)
Jehovah-Tsidkenu, "The Lord, our Righteousness" (Jer. 23:6)
Jehovah-Shalom, "The Lord, our Peace" (Judg. 6:24)
Jehovah-Rohi, "The Lord, our Shepherd" (Ps. 23:1)

> The order here given, is that in which the soul has to learn Jehovah's Name—Sacrifice and Substitute first (Isa. 53); Righteousness is thus revealed, manifested, and declared (Rom. 1:17; 3:21, 25), and the effect to the believing sinner is peace (Isa. 32:17; Rom. 5:1). Thus at peace with God, he returns to the Living Shepherd (Heb. 13:20), who guides him along the heavenward way (1 Peter 2:25).

123   It Pleased God—

To bruise His Son (Isa. 53:10)—In Death
To make all fulness dwell (Col. 1:19)—In Resurrection
To save them that believe (1 Cor. 1:21)—In Grace

124   Three Personal Questions

How long have I to live? (2 Sam. 19:34)—Concern
How long wilt thou sleep? (Prov. 6:9)—Indifference
How long halt ye? (1 Kings 18:21)—Procrastination

125   The Gospel Feast

Feast Provided (Luke 14:16, 17)—Salvation of God
Feast Refused (Luke 14:18-20)—Grace-rejecter
Feast Enjoyed (Luke 14:21-23)—Christ-accepter

126   Bible Scenes

Eden (Gen. 2:8), The Fall of Man—Ruin
Sinai (Exod. 19:18; 20:1), The Law Given—Transgression
Bethlehem (Luke 2:4-16), Savior Born—Incarnation
Calvary (Luke 23:33), Lamb Offered—Redemption
Olivet (Acts 1:9-12), Victor Departs—Ascension

127   Children of God

By *Faith* we become God's Children (Gal. 3:26)
Our *Obedience* proves us God's Childrren (1 Peter 1:14)
Our *Life* manifests we are God's Children (Phil. 2:12)

128   Christ, the Rock

Rock of Salvation (Ps. 89:26)—For the Lost
Rock of Refuge (Ps. 94:22)—For the Exposed
Rock of Rest (Isa. 32:2)—For the Weary
Rock of Refreshment (Isa. 48:21)—For the Thirsty

129 Looking Unto Jesus

Looking unto Jesus (Isa. 45:22)—The Dying One
Looking unto Jesus (Heb. 12:2)—The Glorified One
Looking unto Jesus (Phil. 3:20)—The Coming One

130 Exceeding

Exceeding Sinfulness of Sin (Rom. 7:13)—In Man's Conviction

Exceeding Riches of God's Grace (Eph. 2:7)—In Man's Salvation

Exceeding Greatness of His Power (Eph. 1:19)—In Christ's Resurrection, and ours

Exceeding Weight of Glory (2 Cor. 4:17)—In Saints' Anticipation

131 Seeing Jesus

We *would* see Jesus (John 12:21)—The Awakened One's Desire

We *do* see Jesus (Heb. 2:9)—Experience of Saved

We *shall* see Jesus (1 John 3:2)—Waiting one's Hope

132 Rest

No Rest in Sin (Isa. 57:20)—The Worldling's Want
No Rest in Legality (Lam. 5:5)—The Legalist's Lack
True Rest in Christ (Matt. 11:28)—Believer's Portion
Rest with Christ (Rev. 14:13)—Laborer's Reward

133 Two Pointed Questions

Whence camest thou? (Gen. 16:8)—The Wandering Sinner
Whence came they? (Rev. 7:13, 14)—The Glorified Saints

The *first* question regards man's ruin by sin and departure from God. The *second*, with its answer, tells God's remedy and the sinner's only title to and fitness for Heaven.

134   The Lord Knoweth

Thoughts of Man (Ps. 94:11; 139:2; Heb. 4:12)
Secrets of the Heart (Ps. 44:21; Jer. 17:10; Luke 16:15)
Them that trust in Him (Nah. 1:7; John 10:14; 21:15)
Them that are His (2 Tim. 2:19; 2 Peter 2:2; Ps. 1:6)

135   Darkness

The Unconverted are described in the Word as—

In Darkness (1 John 2:9, 11; John 3:19; Acts 26:18)
They *are* Darkness (Eph. 5:8; Ps. 107:10; Luke 11:35)
They *will be* in the Blackness of Darkness (Jude 13; 2 Peter 2:17)

136   Abundant

Abundant Pardon (Isa. 55:7)—To the Guilty
Abundant Mercy (1 Peter 1:3)—To the Needy
Abundant Grace (1 Tim. 1:14)—To the Sinful
Abundant Peace (Ps. 37:11)—To the Troubled

137   The Saved Sinner's Relation to Christ

Saved *by* Christ (2 Tim. 2:9)—His Place
Sanctified *in* Christ (1 Cor. 1:2)—His Position
Separated *to* Christ (Ps. 4:3)—His Path
Satisfied *with* Christ (Ps. 63:5)—His Portion
Swift *for* Christ (Ps. 147:15)—His Practice

138   Degrees of Faith

No Faith (Mark 4:40)—The Unbeliever
Little Faith (Matt. 16:8)—The Doubter
Growing Faith (2 Thess. 1:3)—The Healthy Believer
Strong Faith (Rom. 4:20)—The Aged Pilgrim
Full of Faith (Acts 6:8)—The Fearless Witness

139   Satisfied

Not satisfied (Eccl. 1:8)—The Sinner in the World
Abundantly satisfied (Ps. 36:8)—Saint's Portion
He shall be satisfied (Isa. 53:11)—Savior's Reward
I shall be satisfied (Ps. 17:15)—Believer's Prospect

140   In Hell

Weeping (Matt. 8:12)—The Sinner's Regret
Wailing (Matt. 13:42)—The Sinner's Remorse
Gnashing Teeth (Luke 13:28)—Sinner's Rebellion

141   Accepted and Acceptable

Accepted Surety (Lev. 1:4)—The Perfect Sacrifice
Accepted Believer (Eph. 1:6)—The Saint's Standing
Acceptable Sacrifice (Rom. 12:1)—Believer's Gift
Acceptable Service (2 Cor. 5:9)—The Believer's Aim

The Cross is the foundation of all. Christ offered to God for man
Faith identifies the believer with Christ, who henceforth is seen *in*
Him
The practical result is devotedness; yielding himself *to* God
The constant aim is to be well-pleasing *unto* God

142   Searching Questions

Where are thou? (Gen. 3:9)—Lost or Saved?
Whose son art thou? (1 Sam. 17:28)—God's or Satan's?
To whom belongest thou? (1 Sam. 30:13)—Christ or the
World?

143   Crowns

Crowned in Innocence (Ps. 8:5)—Man as Created
Crowned in Sin (Lam. 5:16)—Man Fallen
Crowned in Grace (Ps. 103:4)—Man Redeemed
Crowned in Glory (Rev. 4:5)—Man Glorified

144 **Windows**

Jezebel's Window (2 Kings 9:30), The Painted Face—
    Hypocrisy
Rahab's Window (Josh 2:15, 21), Scarlet Line—Redemption
Noah's Window (Gen. 6:16), To Light and Heaven—
    Communion
Daniel's Window (Dan. 6:10)—Prayer and Hope

145 **Altars**

An Altar of Earth (Exod. 20:24)—Atonement
An Altar of Brass (Exod. 26:1-8)—Acceptance
An Altar of Gold (Exod. 30:1-10)—Communion

The sinner's need—the one way to God—The Word made flesh
God's Provision—The Perfect Sacrifice—Christ on the Cross
The Worshiper's Privilege—To draw near—Christ in Heaven

146 **Christ, the Life**

The Source of Life (John 1:4)—"In Him was life"
The Giver of Life (John 10:10)—"I am come that they might
    have life"
The Security of Life (Col. 3:3)—"Your life is hid with
    Christ"
The Sustainer of Life (John 11:57)—"He shall live *by* Me"
The Object of Life (Phil. 1:21)—"For, to me to live is Christ"

147 **Great Things**

Great Sinners (Gen. 6:6)—Measure of Human Guilt
Great Love (Eph. 2:5)—Measure of Divine Love
Great Salvation (Heb. 2:3)—Believer's Deliverance
Great Gulf (Luke 16:26)—Christ-rejecter's Doom

148　　　　　Works

Wicked works (Col. 1:21, with Gal. 5:19; John 7:7)
Dead works (Heb. 9:14, with Heb. 6:1; Rev. 3:1)
Good works (Eph. 2:10, with Titus 3:8; 2 Cor. 9:8)

The first are those of the *natural* man; the second, those of the *religious* man; the third, those of the *converted* man

149　　　　　Saved

By Christ's Death (1 Cor. 1:18)—From Sin's Penalty
By His Risen Life (Rom. 5:10)—From Sin's Practice
At His Coming Again (Heb. 9:28)—From Sin's Presence

150　Three Classes of Gospel Hearers

Professors (Titus 1:16)—Put on without, nothing within
Possessors (1 John 5:9)—Received and enjoyed within
Confessors (Rom. 10:9)—Comes out, because within

151　　Sinner's Three Stages Down
(Jude 11)

"Way of Cain"—The Religious Sinner—Worship without
　　Atonement
"Error of Balaam"—The Worldly Sinner—Love of Money—
　　False Prophet
"Gainsaying of Core"—The Impious Sinner—Priestly
　　Pretensions—End, the Pit

152　　Unconverted Professors Are

Wells without Water (2 Peter 2:17)—Empty and Dry
Trees without Fruit (Jude 12)—Lifeless and Fruitless
Lamps without Oil (Matt. 25:3)—Graceless and Powerless

153   **Three Invitations**

Come and *Drink* (John 7:37)—To the Thirsty
Come and *Rest* (Matt. 11:28)—To the Weary
Come and *See* (John 1:46)—To the Inquiring

154   **Three Circles of Love**

"The World"—"God so loved the *world*" (John 3:16)—
   Inclusive
"The Church"—"Christ loved the *Church*" (Eph. 5:25)—
   Elective
"Me"—"Who loved *Me*" (Gal. 2:20)—Personal

155   **The Mighty One**

Mighty to Redeem (Prov. 23:11)—From Sin's Penalty
Mighty to Save (Isa. 63:1)—From Sin's Power
Mighty to Deliver (Luke 9:43)—From Satan's Possession

156   **Calls of Christ**

Come Down (Luke 19:5)—To the Exalted Sinner
Come Hither (John 4:16)—To the Convicted Sinner
Come Forth (John 11:43)—To the Dead Sinner
Come Out (2 Cor. 6:17)—To the Converted Sinner
Come Away (Song 2:10)—To the Eternal Glory

157   **The Mercy of God**

Great in Mercy (Num. 14:18)—In Forbearance
Rich in Mercy (Eph. 2:4)—In Salvation
Abundant in Mercy (1 Peter 1:3)—In Regeneration
Bounteous in Mercy (Phil. 2:27)—In Preservation

158   **Four Gifts of God**

The Gift of His Son (John 3:16)—To Save the Lost
Of Righteousness (Rom. 5:17)—To Justify the Guilty
Of Eternal Life (Rom. 6:23)—To Raise the Dead
Gift of His Spirit (Acts 15:8)—To Seal the Living

159   What God Hath Made

Made Him to be Sin (2 Cor. 5:21)—Sinless Surety
Made to meet on Him iniquity (Isa. 53:6)—Sinbearer
Made the righteousness of God (2 Cor. 5:21)—Result
Made nigh by blood (Eph. 2:13)—The Perfect Title
Made meet for Heaven (Col. 1:12)—Divine Fitness

160   Three "Excepts"

Except ye Repent (Luke 13:3)—A Godward Change of *Mind*
Except a man be Born Again (John 3:3)—An Inward
    Change of *Nature*
Except ye be Converted (Matt. 18:2)—An Outward Change
    of *Life*

161   God's Description of Man

In Romans 5

"Without Strength" (v. 6)—Man's State
"Ungodly" (v. 6)—Alienation from God—Man's Place
"Sinners" (v. 8)—Activity in Sin—Man's Practice
"Enemies" (v. 10)—Depravity—Man's Position

The root of the tree is below, its branches and fruit above

162   Days

Day of Salvation (2 Cor. 6:2)—Day of Gospel Grace
Day of Privilege (Luke 19:42)—Day of God's Power
Day of Judgment (2 Peter 2:9)—Day of Reckoning
Day of Perdition (2 Peter 3:7)—Day of Doom

163   Found

By Christ (Luke 15:4-6)—As a Wandering Sinner
In Christ (Phil. 3:9)—As a Self Emptied Saint
Of Christ (2 Peter 3:14)—As a Faithful Servant

164 The Glory of God

Come short of it (Rom. 3:23)—The Sinner's State
Christ came to give it (Luke 2:14)—Savior's Aim
The Son manifested it (John 1:14)—Son's Mission
Sinners are saved to it (Rom. 15:7)—Gospel's Object
Rejoice in hope of it (Rom. 5:2)—Believer's Hope
All will yet own it (Phil. 2:11)—The Unbeliever's Prospect

165 Three Offices of Christ

The Propitiation (1 John 2:2, with Rom. 3:25)—To Provide
a Meeting place *with* God
The Purger of Sin (Heb. 1:3, with 9:14)—To Prepare for
the Presence *of* God
The High Priest (Heb. 4:14, with 7:25)—To Represent
His People *before* God

166 Blood and Wrath

The *Blood* of the Lamb (Rev. 7:14)—The Believing Sinner's
Title
The *Wrath* of the Lamb (Rev. 6:16)—The Christless Sinner's
Dread

Atoning Blood procures Heaven for the Believer, and gives him a title
to it.

Righteous Wrath comes upon the sinner, for personal guilt and rejection
of grace.

167 The Name of Jesus

Salvation by His Name (Matt. 1:21)—The Purpose for which
He came
Forgiveness through His Name (Acts 10:43)—The Means
through which it comes
Sonship in His Name (John 1:12)—The Relation to
which it brings
Separation for His Name (Acts 15:14)—The Object for
which it acts

168 Three "Beholds" of Christ

Behold, I stand at the door (Rev. 3:20)—The Word of Entreaty

Behold, now is the day of salvation (2 Cor. 6:2)—The Word of Promise

Behold, I come as a thief (Rev. 16:15)—The Word of Warning

169 Man's Righteousness

Man is unrighteous (Rom. 3:10)

Unfit for God's Kingdom (1 Cor. 6:9)

Seeks to establish his own righteousness (Rom. 10:3)

Holds it fast (Job 27:6)

It is as filthy rags (Isa. 64:6)

Must renounce it for Christ (Phil. 3:9)

170 Threefold Justification

Self-justification (Luke 16:15, with Job 22:2)—The Proud Sinner's Condition

Divine Justification (Rom. 4:5, with Rom. 8:33)—The Believing Sinner's Position

Human Justification (James 2:24, with Micah 6:8)—The Believer's Testimony to Men

171 Four Mighty Words

An *Invitation* to the Weary (Matt. 11:28)

A *Call* to the Thirsty (John 7:37)

A *Promise* to the Sinful (Isa. 1:18)

A *Warning* to the Careless (2 Peter 3:10)

172 Wings

Wings of Salvation (Matt. 23:37)—Cover the Exposed

Wings of Shelter (Ruth 2:12)—To the Trusting Soul

Wings of Strength (Deut. 32:11)—Bear the Weak

Wings of Service (Isa. 40:31)—To Rise to God

173   Divine Love

Unmerited—"Not that we loved God" (1 John 4:10)
Unlimited—"For God so loved the world" (John 3:16)
Undeserved—"God commendeth His love while we were yet
    sinners" (Rom. 5:8)
Unchanging—"I loved thee with an everlasting love" (Jer.
    31:3)

174   What Grace Does

Justified by Grace (Rom. 3:24)—Source of Deliverance
Saved by Grace (Eph. 2:5)—Principle of Salvation
Standing in Grace (Rom. 5:2)—Ground of Access
Singing with Grace (Col. 3:16)—Motive for Praise
Serving in Grace (Heb. 12:28)—The Spring of Work

175   Five Relationships With Christ

To Christ (John 6:37)—For Salvation
In Christ (Rom. 8:1)—Free from Condemnation
On Christ (1 Peter 2:6)—As a Sure Foundation
With Christ (John 13:8)—As a Saint in Communion
Unto Christ (Acts 1:8)—As a Witness in Testimony

176   Ears

Ears Open (Job 36:10)—To Hear God's Word
Ears to Hear (Mark 4:9)—To Receive its Message
Ears Turned Away (2 Tim. 4:4)—By False Teachers
Ears Closed (Acts 28:27)—Prejudice and Unbelief
Ears Stopped (Acts 7:57)—In opposition and Rejection

177   Four Present Possessions

Pardon—"He will abundantly pardon" (Isa. 55:7)
Peace—"He is our peace" (Eph. 2:14)
Purity—"To purify unto Himself" (Titus 2:14)
Power—"He giveth power" (Isa. 40:29; 2 Tim.
    1:7)

178 Everlasting Things

Everlasting Love (Jer. 31:3)—Of God to all
Everlasting Righteousness (Ps. 119:142)—For all
Everlasting Covenant (Heb. 13:20)—Including all
Everlasting Salvation (Isa. 45:17)—Proclaimed to all
Everlasting Life (John 3:16)—Possessed by all Believers

179 Ready

The Sinner is "ready to perish" (Isa. 27:13)
God is "ready to pardon" (Neh. 9:17)
Salvation is "ready to be revealed" (1 Peter 1:5)
The Son of Man is "ready to judge" (1 Peter 4:5)
    "Be ye also ready"

180 Blessed Is the Man—

Whose transgression is forgiven (Ps. 32:1)
Whose strength is in Thee (Ps. 84:5)
Who maketh the Lord his trust (Ps. 40:4)
That heareth Me (Prov. 8:34)
That walketh not in counsel of ungodly (Ps. 1:1)

181 Truth in Two Aspects

Clean (John 15:3)—Being cleansed (2 Cor. 7:1)
Sanctified (1 Cor. 6:9)—Being sanctified (John 17:17)
Kept (1 Peter 1:5)—Keep yourselves (Jude 21)

      All true absolutely of all believers *in* Christ
      All being fulfilled *in* them progressively

182 Jesus, the Savior

A Savior (Luke 2:11)—General
The Savior (John 4:42)—Solitary
Our Savior (Titus 1:4)—Personal
My Savior (Luke 1:47)—Individual

183   No Neutrality

Cannot serve God and Mammon (Matt. 6:24)
Cannot partake with Christ and devils (1 Cor. 10:21)
Cannot live to self and be Christ's Disciple (Luke 14:26)

184   Three Great Life Truths

Regeneration (Titus 3:5)—Life Originated
Restoration (Ps. 23:2)—Life Maintained
Resurrection (1 Cor. 15:22)—Life Victorious

185   Two Visages

The *Sinner's* Visage Blackened (Lam. 4:8)—*By* sin
The *Savior's* Visage Marred (Isa. 52:14)—*For* sin

186   Three Symbols of Christ's Work

As a *Lamb* He redeems (1 Peter 1:19)
As a *Hen* He covers (Matt. 23:37)
As an *Eagle* He carries (Deut. 32:11)

187   Tokens

Token of Safety (Exod. 12:13)—The Blood
Token of Security (Josh. 2:12)—The Word
Token of Perdition (Phil. 1:28)—The Judgment

188   The Word Is Able

To Make Wise (2 Tim. 3:15)—The Young
To Save (James 1:21)—The Lost
To Build Up (Acts 20:32)—The Saved

189   Two Hard Things

The way of transgressors is *hard* (Prov. 13:15)
Thy wrath lieth *hard* upon me (Ps. 88:7)

  The former is the result of man's sin, the latter the suffering of the Sinbearer.

190   Three "Past" Things

Past Life in Sin (Eph. 2:2)—The Believer
Past Feeling (Eph. 4:19)—The Hardened Sinner
Past Harvest (Jer. 8:20)—The Grace Despiser

191   Four Houses

House of Bondage (Deut. 5:6)—In Sin
House of Redemption (Exod. 12:13-20)—By Blood
House of Salvation (Acts 16:33-34)—Through Grace
House of Glory (John 14:2)—In Heaven

192   Threefold Victory

Victory over Sin (Rom. 6:14)—By Grace
Victory over Satan (1 John 2:14)—By the Word
Victory over the World (1 John 5:4)—By Faith

193   Four Confessions

"I have sinned against the Lord" (2 Sam. 12:13)
"I abhor myself and repent" (Job 42:6)
"I trust in the mercy of God" (Ps. 52:8)
"I know whom I have believed" (2 Tim. 1:12)

194   The Believer's Sins Are—

Borne by the Lord Jesus (1 Peter 2:24)
Removed as far as east from west (Ps. 103:12)
Cast behind God's back (Isa. 38:17)
Into the depths of the sea (Mic. 7:19)
Remembered no more (Heb. 10:17)

195   The Son of God

In Gethsemane (Matt. 26:36)—Betrayed
At Gabbatha (John 19:13)—Delivered
On Golgotha (John 19:17)—Crucified

196   Three Typical Men

Adam the Natural Man (Gen. 3)—Ruin
Abel the Offerer of Sacrifice (Gen. 4)—Redemption
Enoch the Walker with God (Gen. 5)—Communion

197   Three Conditions

Blacker than Coal (Lam. 4:8)—By Nature
Red like Crimson (Isa. 1:18))—In Practice
White as Snow (Isa. 1:18)—Through Grace

198   Our God

God of Great Kindness (Neh. 9:17)—To All
God of Salvation (Ps. 65:5)—From the Past
God of Peace (Phil. 4:9)—For the Present
God of Hope (Rom. 15:13)—To the Future
God of Glory (Acts 7:2)—In Heaven

199   Infinite Realities

The Love of Christ passeth knowledge (Eph. 3:19)
The Riches of Christ are unsearchable (Eph. 3:8)
The Peace of God passeth understanding (Phil. 4:7)
The Ways of God are past finding (Rom. 11:33)

200   With All the Heart

Seeking the Lord (Deut. 4:29)—Anxiety
Trusting in the Lord (Prov. 3:5)—Faith
Turning to the Lord (Deut. 30:10)—Conversion
Obeying the Lord (Deut. 30:2)—Discipleship
Serving the Lord (Deut. 10:12)—Devotion

201   Gospel Signals

Danger—"Flee from the wrath to come" (Matt. 3:7)
Caution—"Boast not...of tomorrow" (Prov. 27:1)
Safety—"Salvation is of the Lord" (Jonah 2:9)

202 No Difference

In *Nature*—There is no difference (Rom. 3:22)
In *Grace*—There is no difference (Rom. 10:12)

203 The Lord's Joy in Saving Sinners Is—

As the Shepherd's over His Sheep (Luke 15:7)
As the Buyer's in His Treasure (Matt. 13:44)
As the Bridegroom's over His Bride (Isa. 62:5)
As the Reaper's over His Sheaves (Ps. 126:6)

204 The Work of Christ

Christ *died* to redeem (Titus 2:14)
He *rose* to justify (Rom. 4:25)
He *lives* to save (Heb. 7:25)
He *comes* to glorify (Col. 3:4)

205 Conversion

God (1 Thess. 1:9)—The Author and Object
Through the Word (Ps. 19:7)—The Means
By the Soul-winner (James 5:19)—The Instrument
The man himself (Acts 3:19)—The Subject

206 Daily Things in the Early Church

Sinners daily saved (Acts 2:47)
Churches daily multiplied (Acts 16:5)
Scriptures daily searched (Acts 16:11)
Saints daily persecuted (1 Cor. 15:31)

207 Persuading

We persuade men (2 Cor. 5:11)—Preacher's Business
Almost persuaded (Acts 26:28)—The Procrastinator
Never persuaded (Luke 16:31)—The Hardened
I am persuaded (Rom. 8:38, 39)—The Christian

GOSPEL TRUTHS

208   God's Salvation

And Things That Accompany It

The *Author* of Salvation (Heb. 5:9)
The *Gospel* of Salvation (Eph. 1:13)
The *Way* of Salvation (Acts 16:17)
The *Knowledge* of Salvation (Luke 1:77)
The *Joy* of Salvation (Ps. 51:12)
The *Hope* of Salvation (1 Thess. 5:8)

209   The Divinity of Christ

The Father affirmed it (Matt. 3:17)—From Heaven
Demons acknowledged it (Mark 3:11)—From Hell
The Disciples confessed it (Matt. 16:16)—In Faith
The Centurion avowed it (Matt. 27:54)—In Fear
The Apostles proclaimed it (Acts 9:20)—In Power
The Sinner believes it (John 20:31)—Unto Salvation

210   The Sufferings of Christ

He suffered for sins—At the hand of God (1 Peter 3:18)
He suffered for righteousness—From men (1 Peter 2:23)
He suffered, being tempted—From Satan (Heb. 2:18)

211   The Savior

A Savior Promised (Isa. 19:20)
A Savior Born (Luke 2:11)
A Savior Sent (1 John 4:14)
A Savior Received (John 1:12)
A Savior Rejected (John 12:48)

212 Two Meeting Places

The Mercyseat (Exod. 25:21, 22)—Grace
The Great White Throne (Rev. 20:11)—Judgment
  All must meet God at the one or the other

213 Cleansing

Man's Natural State (Isa. 64:6; Ps. 51:5-7)
No Cleansing by Man's Efforts (Jer. 2:22; Job 9:30)
Atonement, the Ground of it (Lev. 16:30; Heb. 1:3)
Effected once for all (Heb. 10:12; John 15:3)
The Continuous Efficacy of the Blood (1 John 1:7)
Daily Cleansing by the Word (Eph. 5:26; Ps. 119:9)

214 Christ and His Own

Christ sacrificed *for* us (1 Cor. 5:7)—On the Cross
Christ accepted *by* us (John 1:12)—By Faith
Christ formed *in* us (Gal. 4:19)—By Regeneration
Christ manifested *to* us (John 14:22)—In Communion
Christ coming *with* us (Col. 3:4)—At His Appearing

215 Opened Things

Opened *Fountain* (Zech. 13:1—Cleansing by Christ
Opened *Heart* (Acts 16:14)—For Person of Christ
Opened *Understanding* (Luke 24:45)—For the Word
Opened *Book* (Luke 24:32)—To unfold Christ's glories
Opened *Mouth* (Eph. 6:19)—To Testify for Christ

216 Children

Children of Wrath (Eph. 2:3)—By Nature (Rom. 5:12)
Children of Disobedience (Eph. 2:2)—By Practice (Isa. 53:6)
Children of the Devil (John 8:44)—By Manifestation (see
  1 John 3:8-10)
Children of God (Gal. 3)—By Faith (see 1 John 3:1, 2)

217   Whom Jesus Saves

Came to save Sinners (1 Tim. 1:15)
Came to call Sinners (Matt. 9:13)
Died for Sinners (Rom. 5:8)
Receiveth Sinners (Luke 15:2)

218   The Righteousness of God

Declared at the Cross (Rom. 3:26, with Ps. 85:10)
Revealed in the Gospel (Rom. 1:17, with 3:21; 10:10)
Imputed to Believers (Rom. 4:6; Heb. 11:4; 1 Cor. 1:30)
Rejected by Legalists (Rom. 10:3; Luke 18:9; Titus 3:5)

219   Heaven and Hell Opened

Heaven opened to Jesus (Luke 3:21)
The Grave opened by Jesus (Matt. 27:51)
Heaven opened to Saints (Acts 7:55)
Hell opened for Sinners (Isa. 5:14)

220   A Sevenfold Confession

"I am vile" (Job 40:4)—The Confession of Sin
"I am undone" (Isa. 6:5)—Cry of Conscious Guilt
"I am a sinful man" (Luke 5:8)—Cry of Conviction
"I am not worthy" (Matt. 8:8)—Confession of Emptiness
"I am poor and needy" (Ps. 40:17)—Cry of Need
"I am Thine, save me" (Ps. 119:94)—The Call of Faith
"I am black, but comely" (Song 1:5)—Condition of saints

221   The Word of God:

Its Action on the Unconverted

Hammer to Break (Jer. 23:29)—Conscience Reached
A Sword to Smite (Heb. 4:12)—The Inwards Searched
A Fire to Melt (Jer. 23:29)—Heart made Tender
A Mirror to Show (James 1:25)—The State Revealed

222   The Word of God:

Its Effects on the Believer

Seed to Give Life (1 Peter 1:23)—Receive it (James 1:21)
Water to Cleanse (Eph. 5:26)—Use it (Ps. 119:9, 10)
Bread to Strengthen (Jer. 15:16)—Eat it (Ps. 1:2)
Light to Guide (Ps. 119:105)—Walk in it (1 John 1:7)

223   Righteousness in Four Aspects

(Romans 10)

Man's Righteousness (v. 3)—Human
The Righteousness of the Law (v. 4)—Condemning
The Righteousness of God (v. 3)—Justifying
The Righteousness of Faith (v. 6)—Appropriating

224   Threefold View of Christ

Christ on the Cross (John 19:17-19)—Dying
Christ on the Throne (Heb. 10:12)—Living
Christ in the Heart (Eph. 3:17)—Indwelling

225   Peace, False and True

No Peace (Isa. 57:21)—The Result of Sin
False Peace (Jer. 6:14)—The Work of Satan
Way of Peace Unknown (Rom. 3:17)—Ignorance of Man
Basis of Peace (Col. 1:20)—Work of Christ
Gospel of Peace (Eph. 6:15)—Word of Reconciliation
The Reception of Peace (Rom. 5:1)—Result of Faith
The Enjoyment of Peace (Rom. 15:13)—The Saint's Portion

226   Christ's Atonement

Its Necessity (Heb. 9:22)—Foreshadowed in Lev. 16:10, 19
Its Sufficiency (Heb. 9:11, 12)—Attested in Luke 23:45
Its Efficacy (Heb. 9:12)—Proved in Rom. 3:26; 8:34
Its Results (Col. 1:20)—Manifested by Eph. 2:13
Its Rejection (Heb. 10:26-29)—Warned of in Jude 11

227   The Gospel

The Gospel of God (Rom. 1:1)—Its Source
The Gospel of Christ (Rom. 1:16)—Its Subject
The Gospel of your Salvation (Eph. 1:13)—Its Object

228   Fundamental Truths

Ruin by Adam's Fall (Rom. 5:12-16; 1 Cor. 15:22)
Redemption by Christ's Death (Eph. 1:7; Heb. 9:12)
Reception by Faith (John 1:12; 1 John 5:1)
Regeneration by the Holy Spirit (John 3:5; Titus 3:5)
Rejection in Unbelief (John 3:18; 2 Thess. 2:10)

229   The Throne and the Altar

(Isaiah 6:1-8)

Light from the Throne (v. 1)—Conviction and Confession
Live Coal from the Altar (v. 6)—Cleansing and Conversion

The sinner must first know the light of the throne, before he will appreciate the grace of the altar

230   The Heart

A Dark Heart (Rom. 1:21)—In Nature
A Hard Heart (Matt. 19:8)—By Sin
A Tender Heart (2 Kings 22:19)—Through Grace
An Open Heart (Acts 16:14)—By the Spirit
A Clean Heart (1 Peter 1:22)—Through Regeneration
A True Heart (Heb. 10:22)—By Faith

231   Swords

Of Justice (Gen. 3:24)—Set up to exclude Sinners
Of Judgment (Zech. 13:7)—Sheathed in Substitute
Of Defense (Eph. 6:17)—The Saint's Weapon
Of Judgment (Rev. 19:16)—The Sinner's Doom

232 The End

The end of all flesh (Gen. 6:13)—The Sin of Man
End of the age (Heb. 9:26)—The Work of Christ
End of all things (1 Peter 4:7)—The Eternal Future

233 Bible Plants

Bleeding Myrrh (Song 5:5)—The Dying Savior
Lowly Hyssop (1 Kings 4:23)—Emblem of Faith
The Lovely Lily (Song 2:2)—The Beauty of Saints
Prickly Thorn (Heb. 6:8)—The Condemned Sinner

234 Lamps

Lamps without Oil (Matt. 25:3)—Empty Profession
Lamps with Oil (Matt. 25:4)—True Conversion
Lamps in Pitchers (Judg. 7:16)—Bright Confession
Lamps well Trimmed (Lev. 24:2)—Right Condition

235 Great Foundation Truths

Ruin in Sin (Rom. 5:12)
Redemption by the Blood of Christ (Eph. 1:7)
Regeneration by the Holy Spirit (John 3:5)
Resurrection of the Dead (John 5:28, 29)

236 Bible Birds

Bird of Sacrifice (Lev. 14:4)—The Sparrow
Bird of Peace (Gen. 8:9)—The Dove
Bird of Power (Deut. 33:11)—The Eagle

The order is that in which the soul needs and apprehends the Truth.
All are types of Christ.

237 Israel's Food

The Lamb in Egypt (Exod. 12:11)—Christ on the Cross
Manna in Wilderness (Num. 10:9)—Christ on Earth
Old Corn in Canaan (Josh 5:10)—Christ in Heaven

238   Five Baptisms

Christ's Baptism of Suffering (Luke 12:50)—Atonement
John's Baptism of Repentance (Mark 1:4)—Confession
Believer's Baptism (Matt. 28:19)—Obedience
Baptism of the Spirit (1 Cor. 12:13)—Unity
Baptism with Fire (Matt. 3:11, 12)—Judgment

239   Redemption

Obtained *for* us (Heb. 9:12)—At the Cross
Sent *to* us (Ps. 111:9)—In the Gospel
Known *by* us (1 Cor. 1:30)—In the Present
Accomplished *in* us (Rom. 8:23)—In the Future

240   Sin: Its Pleasure and Punishment

Pleasures of Sin (Heb. 11:25)—The Choice
Deceitfulness of Sin (Heb. 3:13)—The Process
Wages of Sin (Rom. 6:23)—The Result
Punishment of Sin (Matt. 25:46)—The Retribution

241   Bond-servants

Bond-servants of Sin (John 8:34)—By Nature
Bond-servants of Satan (Acts 26:18)—By Conquest
Bond-servants of Christ (Rom. 1:1)—By Grace

242   Windows of Heaven

Opened in Judgment (Gen. 6:11)—Man's Sin
Closed by Unbelief (2 Kings 7:2)—Man's Unbelief
Opened in Blessing (Mal. 3:10)—God's Grace

243   Condemnation

Condemned (Rom. 5:18)—By Nature
Not Condemned (John 3:18)—Through Grace
No Condemnation (Rom. 8:1)—In Christ

244 Forgiveness

The Need of it (Mark 2:7)—Sin
The Cause of it (Eph. 4:32)—For Christ's Sake
The Proclamation of it (Acts 13:38)—Be it known
The Extent of it (Col. 2:13)—All trespasses
The Knowledge of it (1 John 2:12)—Are
The Object of it (Ps. 130:4)—Fear of God

245 Jesus Christ, the Shepherd

Psalms 22, 23, and 24 describe Him thus

The Good Shepherd (John 10:11)—Who Died for us
The Great Shepherd (Heb. 13:20)—Who Lives for us
The Chief Shepherd (1 Peter 5:3)—Who will come for us

246 Jesus Christ, the Lord

Exalted by God as Lord (Acts 2:36)
Confessed by the Believer (Rom. 10:9)
Owned and Obeyed (Acts 9:6; Col. 3:17)
Served and Honored (Col. 3:24)

247 Jesus Christ, Faith's Object

Looking *unto* Jesus (Heb. 12:2)—Our Savior
Learning *of* Jesus (Luke 10:39)—Our Teacher
Leaning *on* Jesus (Song 8:5)—Our Strength
Looking *for* Jesus (Phil. 3:20)—Our Hope

248 Sin, Sacrifice, Salvation

The Sin of Man *brings* death *on* all (Rom. 5:12)
The Sacrifice of Christ is *for* all (1 Tim. 2:6)
The Salvation of God is brought *unto* all (Titus 2:11)

249 God's Riches

Of His Goodness (Rom. 2:4)—Leads to Repentance
Riches of His Grace (Eph. 1:7)—Forgives our Sins
Of His Glory (Rom. 9:23)—Prepares for Heaven

250 Cleansed, Clothed, Crowned

Cleansed from Sin (Rev. 1:5)—By the Blood
Clothed in Righteousness (Phil. 3:9)—In the Person
Crowned with Glory (Rev. 4:4)—On the Throne

The former two are known on earth; the last in Heaven

251 Life, Light, Liberty

Life in and from Christ by Faith (John 1:4; 3:36)
Light from Christ through the Word (John 8:12; Ps. 119:11)
Liberty in Christ, in us by the Spirit (John 8:36; Gal. 5:1;
2 Cor. 3:17)

252 Three Gospel R's

Repentance, change of mind toward God (Acts 20:21)
Regeneration, new life from God (Titus 3:5)
Reconciliation, new relationship with God (2 Cor. 5:20)

253 Always Ready

Ready to Die (2 Tim. 4:6)
Ready to Preach (Rom. 1:15)
Ready to Testify (1 Peter 3:15)
Ready for Christ's Coming (Matt. 25:10)

254 Christ's Lordship

Avowed by Professors (Matt. 7:21)
Denied by False Teachers (Jude 4)
Confessed by His Servants (Phil. 3:8)
To be Ackowledged by All (Phil. 2:9)

255 Refuges

Refuge of Lies (Isa. 28:15)—The Self-righteous
Refuge in the Gospel (Heb. 6:18)—Convicted Sinner
Refuge in God (Ps. 46:1)—The Believing Sinner

256   Our Names

Sinners (Rom. 5:19; 1 Tim. 1:15)—By Nature and Practice
Saints (Rom. 1:7; Eph. 5:3)—By Call and Conduct
Sons (1 John 3:1; Phil. 2:15)—By Birth and Testimony
Servants (Acts 27:23; John 12:26)—By Purchase and Obedience

257   Guilt, Grace, Glory

Man's Guilt (Rom. 5:14)—Brings Condemnation
God's Grace (Titus 2:11)—Brings Salvation
Christ's Glory (John 17:22, 24)—Gives Exaltation

258   God Is—

The God of Salvation (Hab. 3:18)
The God of Peace (Phil. 4:9)
The God of Patience (Rom. 15:5)
The God of Hope (Rom. 15:13)
The God of Glory (Acts 7:2)

In this order, men know God and learn of Him

259   God's "Musts"

Ye must be Born Again (John 3:7)—Man's Necessity
The Son must die (John 3:14)—God's Provision
We must be saved (Acts 4:12)—Believer's Certainty

260   Man's Photograph—

In Nature	In Grace
Head (Isa. 1:5)	Head (Ps. 23:5)
Eyes (Acts 28:27)	Eyes (John 9:25)
Mouth (Rom. 3:14)	Mouth (Ps. 40:3)
Ears (Matt. 13:15)	Ears (John 10:27)
Hands (Mic. 7:3)	Hands (Eph. 4:28)
Feet (Rom. 3:15)	Feet (Eph. 6:15)

261 Grace and Judgment
(Proverbs 1:24-26)

God Calling (v. 24)—Grace
Man Refusing (v. 24)—Impenitence
God Laughing (v. 6)—Judgment
Man Fearing (v. 26)—Remorse

262 Safe, Sure, Satisfied

Safe *in* Christ (John 10:9)—The Believer's Salvation
Sure *by* Christ (John 10:28)—The Believer's Certainty
Satisfied *with* Christ (Song 2:3)—Believer's Enjoyment

263 Man's History

In Nature	In Grace
My Birth (Ps. 51:5)	My Birthday (1 John 5:1)
My Character (Titus 3:3)	My Life (Rom. 6:4)
My Path (Rom. 3:16)	My Food (1 Peter 2:2)
My Conduct (Eph. 2:2)	My Growth (2 Peter 3:18)
My Company (Rom. 1:20)	My Lessons (Titus 3:14)
My Prospects (Heb. 10:27)	My Teacher (Matt. 11:29)
My Destiny (Matt. 7:13)	My Home (John 14:3)

264 Christ, the Stone

A Tried Stone (Isa. 28:16)—In Life
A Foundation Stone (1 Cor. 3:11)—In Death
A Living Stone (1 Peter 2:4)—In Resurrection
A Corner Stone (Eph. 2:20)—In Ascension
A Head Stone (1 Peter 2:7)—In Glory
A Falling Stone (Matt. 21:44)—In Judgment

265 The Blood and the Hyssop
(Exodus 12:22)

The Blood in the Basin—Christ's Death
The Hyssop in the Hand—Faith's Appropriation

266 Saved and Being Saved

Believers *are* saved Eternally (Acts 16:31; 2 Tim. 1:9)—
Christ's Finished Work
Believers are *being* saved Daily (Rom. 5:10; Heb. 7:25)—
Christ's Unfinished Work

267 Doors

Door of Salvation (John 10:9)—The Way of Life
Door of Communion (Matt. 6:6)—Source of Strength
Door of Service (Rev. 3:8)—Privilege of Servants
Door of Glory (Rev. 4:1)—The Hope of Saints
Door of Mercy (Luke 13:25)—Doom of Rejectors

268 Let Alone

Let *them* alone (Matt. 15:14)—False Teachers
Let *it* alone (Luke 13:8)—Fruitless Professors
Let *him* alone (Hosea 4:17)—Hardened Sinners

269 Weighed

Actions weighed (1 Sam. 2:3)—Man's Works
Spirits weighed (Prov. 16:2)—Man's Motives
Thou art weighed (Dan. 5:27)—Man's Person

270 Things Exceeding

Man's Exceeding Sin (Gen. 13:13)
God's Exceeding Grace (Eph. 2:7)
Christ's Exceeding Sorrow (Matt. 26:38)
Believer's Exceeding Joy (1 Peter 4:13)

271 True Tokens

Token of Salvation (Exod. 12:13)—The Blood
Token of Judgment Past (Gen. 9:12)—The Bow
Token of Security (Josh. 2:12)—The Scarlet Cord
Token of Relationship (Exod. 13:16)—Word of God

272   A New Creation

Demanded by God (Gal. 6:15)
Effected in Christ (2 Cor. 5:17)
Manifested by the Spirit (Eph. 2:10)

273   Salvation:

Present—Progressive—Prospective

Salvation already in Possession (1 Cor. 15:2)
Salvation in Progress (Rom. 5:10)
Salvation in Prospect (Rom. 13:11)

274   The Work of Righteousness

(Isaiah 32:17, 18)

The Work of Righteousness (Rom. 5:18)
Peace, the Result (Col. 1:20)
Quietness, the Effect (Matt. 11:28)
Assurance, the Enjoyment (2 Tim. 1:12)

275   Thou and Thy House

Noah (Gen. 7:1)—Invited to Salvation
Cornelius (Acts 10:22; 11:14)—Hearing of Salvation
Jailer (Acts 16:31-34)—Rejoicing in Salvation

276   Full Assurance

Full Assurance of Faith (Heb. 10:22)—The Past
Full Assurance of Understanding (Col. 2:2)—Present
Full Assurance of Hope (Heb. 6:11)—The Future

277   Man's Way and Christ

(Jude 11, with John 14:6)

"*Way* of Cain—Contrast "I am the *Way*"
"*Error* of Balaam"—Contrast "And the *Truth*"
"*Perishing* of Core"—Contrast "And the *Life*"

278   Blood and Water

(John 19:34)

Blood to Atone (Lev. 17:11; Rom. 3:25; Heb. 9:12)
Water to Cleanse (Num. 19:18; John 13:10; Eph. 5:26)

279   Whom God Justifies

"The Ungodly" (Rom. 4:5)—The Character
"That Worketh Not" (Rom. 4:5)—The Condition
"But Believeth" (Rom. 3:26)—The Principle

280   The Sower, the Seed, the Soil

(Luke 8:4-15)

The Sower (v. 5)—The Preacher (Ps. 126:5, 6)
The Seed (v. 11)—The Word (1 Peter 1:23; 2 Tim. 4:4)
The Soil (vv. 12, 13)—The Hearers (Rom. 10:17)
Results (vv. 13, 15)—Indifference, Profession, Salvation

281   Difficulties Solved

Solomon told her all her questions (1 Kings 10:3)
"How can I be sure Christ died for me?" (Rom. 5:6)
"Must I not seek it?" (Luke 19:10)
"I have tried to believe, but cannot" (Rom. 10:9)
"If I could only feel it" (Rom. 15:13)
"I fear I could not hold on" (John 10:28)

The Scriptures given solve the difficulties

282   Profit and Loss

(Mark 8:36)

The World gained, to pass away (1 John 2:17)
The Soul lost, and the loss eternal (Mark 9:43-48)

283   Two "Whosoevers"

The "Whosoever" of Salvation (John 3:16)
The "Whosoever" of Damnation (Rev. 20:15)

284 Two Kinds of Fools

Fools for the Devil and the World (Luke 12:20)
Fools for Christ's Sake (1 Cor. 4:10)

285 Refuges of Lies

(Isaiah 28:15-17)

"God is merciful" (Heb. 10:28)
"No worse than my neighbors" (2 Cor. 10:12)
"We must wait God's time" (2 Cor. 6:2)
"If I am one of the elect" (1 Tim. 2:4)
"There is mercy at the eleventh hour" (Prov. 27:1)

The Scriptures quoted, demolish the false refuges into which the devil seeks to lure sinners

286 From Death to Life

In Death (Eph. 2:1)—The Sinner's State
Life Provided (Rom. 6:23)—God's Free Gift
Life Imparted (John 3:36)—Faith's Reception
From Death to Life (John 5:24)—The New Position

287 Two Masters and Their Servants

(Matthew 6:24)

Christ (John 13:13; Acts 9:6; 27:23)
The Devil (John 13:2; 1 John 3:10; 2 Peter 2:19)
The Servants (John 8:44; 1 John 3:8)
The Wages (Rev. 20:10; Matt. 25:41; John 12:26)

288 From the Pit to the Crown

In the Pit (Isa. 24:22)—Sin
Out of the Pit (Ps. 40:2)—Grace
Set on a Rock (Ps. 40:2)—Safety
Set among Princes (1 Sam. 2:8)—Dignity
Occupying the Throne (1 Sam. 2:8)—Glory

289   Stumbling Blocks Removed

"Take up the stumbling blocks out of the way" (Isa. 57:14)
Working out my own Salvation (Phil. 2:12)
Waiting for the Spirit (Acts 7:51)
Not the right kind of Faith (Heb. 11:1)
Would it not be presumption? (1 John 5:10)

   The Scriptures quoted remove these stumbling blocks

290   Popular Delusions

"Delusion, that they should believe a lie" (2 Thess. 2:11)
"There is no God" (Ps. 14:1)
"No one can know the future" (2 Peter 3:5)
"Man is not immortal" (Luke 12:5)
"The Bible is not reliable" (Prov. 30:5)
"All will be saved at last (Rev. 21:8)

291   Doubts Dispelled

"Dissolving of Doubts" (Dan. 5:12)
"I have been too great a sinner" (Matt. 9:13)
"Is there salvation for me?" (1 Tim. 1:15)
"How could I keep from sinning?" (Rom. 8:2)
"Might I not fall away?" (1 Peter 1:4)

292   Excuses Exploded

"They all with one consent began to make excuses" (Luke
   14:18)
"I don't make any profession" (Ps. 9:17)
"There are so many hypocrites" (Rom. 14:12)
"Many good people can't say they're saved" (Rom. 10:2)
"I'm doing the best I can" (Eph. 2:8)
"There's time enough yet" (Prov. 27:1)

293   Common Proverbs

"As sure as death" (Heb. 9:27)
"Gone to the majority" (Matt. 7:13)
"Make the best of both worlds" (Matt. 6:24)
"Look before you leap" (Prov. 22:3)
"Give the devil his due" (Rev. 20:10)

Goliath was beheaded with his own sword; so these proverbs may be used to bring God's truth home to men of the world

294   The Life Look
(Isaiah 45:22)

The Condition—"Look"
The Object—"Unto Me"
The Result—"Be ye Saved"
The Invited—"All the ends of the earth"

295   Slightly Healed
(Jeremiah 6:13-15)

Covetous People (v. 13)—Like Judas (Matt 26:15)
Baptized Professors (v. 13)—Like Simon (Acts 8:20)
False Preachers (v. 13)—Like Balaam (2 Peter 2:15)
Deceived souls (v. 14)—Christless professors (Rev. 20:10)
Rude Awakening (v. 15)—In Judgment (Luke 16:26-28)

296   The Swelling of Jordan
(Jeremiah 12:1-17)

Footmen and Horsemen—Living and dying without God
Peace in Sin—Trust in self and false refuges
(Joshua 3:14-17)

Jordan's Swelling—Death in all its power to sinners
Jordan Dried—Death abolished by the Savior for the saint
(2 Tim. 1:10)

297 Two Night Visits

(1 Samuel 28:7; John 3:1)

Saul in his distress went to the witch of Endor
Nicodemus in his anxiety went to Jesus

The King, afraid of God, invoked the aid of hell, and perished
The Ruler came to the Light, heard the Gospel, and was saved

298 Two Prodigals

Under *Law* (Deut. 21:20)—Expelled, condemned, stoned
Under *Grace* (Luke 15:11-24)—Received and forgiven

299 Rest in Varied Aspects

Creation Rest (Gen. 2:2)—Marred by Sin
Canaan Rest (Josh. 11:23)—Broken by disobedience
Redemption Rest (Zeph. 3:17)—Secured by Christ
Eternal Rest (Heb. 4:9)—Of God and His People

300 Six Foundation Truths

In Three Pairs: Hebrews 6:1, 2

Repentance and Faith; Relation to God and Christ (Acts
   20:21)

Washings and Sacrifice; Figures of Christ's Sacrifice and
   the Spirit's Work

Resurrection and Eternal Judgment; The Future of Saint
   and Sinner

301 The Glorious Gospel of the Blessed God

(1 Timothy 1:11)

A *Full* Gospel—Christ and nothing *less*
A *Plain* Gospel—Christ and nothing *more*
A *Pure* Gospel—Christ and nothing *else*

302　　　Results of the Cross

(Matthew 27:51-53)

A rent Veil (v. 51)—Heaven Opened

An Open Grave (v. 52)—Death Vanquished

A Risen Savior (v. 53)—God Satisfied

303　　The Preacher and His Message

(Isaiah 61:1-11)

The Prepared Preacher—"Anointed me to preach" (Acts 10:38)

The Divine Message—"Good tidings" (Luke 2:10; Acts 13:32)

The Great Deliverance—"Liberty to the Captives" (Rom. 1:16; John 8:36)

The Favored Time—"The Acceptable Year" (Luke 4:19; 2 Cor. 6:2)

304　　The Watchman's Message

(Isaiah 21:11, 12)

The Scoffer's Question—"Watchman, what of the night?" (2 Peter 3:1)

Morning of Glory—"Morning cometh" (Rev. 22:16)

Night of Judgment—"Also the night" (1 Thess. 5:2)

The Invitation of Grace—"Return" (Chaldee, "Be Converted"), "Come"

305　　　　Two Hours

(John 5:23-29)

The Hour of Life-giving (v. 25)—Present

The Hour of Judgment (v. 28)—Future

　　All must meet the Lord in either of these periods

306　　　Twofold Cleansing

Cleansing by Blood (1 John 1:7)—Before God

Cleansing by Water (Eph. 5:26)—Before Men

307　　　　Times and Seasons

Time of Love (Ezek. 16:8)—The Gospel Age
Time of Visitation (Luke 19:44)—Revival Seasons
Time of Judgment (Rev. 11:18)—Coming Vengeance

308　　　　Opened and Closed

The Door Opened (Acts 14:27)—Grace
The Book Closed (Luke 4:20)—Forbearance
The Door Closed (Luke 13:25)—Grace Ended
The Book Opened (Rev. 6:1)—Judgment Begun

309　　　　Reconciliation

(2 Corinthians 5:18-21)

Its Source—God (Job 33:24)
Its Character—Unto Himself (Col. 1:21)
Its Basis—The Cross (Rom. 5:9)
Its Object—Sinners, Enemies (Rom. 5:10)

310　　　　Peace, Pattern, Power

Christ my *Peace* (Eph. 2:14)—In Heaven
Christ my *Pattern* (1 Peter 2:21)—On Earth
Christ my *Power* (2 Cor. 12:9)—In me

311 The Strong Man and the Stronger

(Luke 11:21, 22)

The Strong Man—Satan (Rev. 12:9)
His Palace—The World (John 14:30; 16:33)
His Goods—The Sinner (Luke 8:27, 30)
The Stronger—The Lord Jesus (1 John 3:8)
Overcame Him—In the Wilderness (Matt. 4:1-11)
Taketh from him his armor—At the Cross (Heb. 2:14, 15)
Divideth his spoils—At Conversion (Acts 26:18)

312   Only One

One God (Mark 12:29)—No Idolatry
One Mediator (1 Tim. 2:5)—No Priestcraft
One Savior (Isa. 45:21)—No Mixtures
One Offering (Heb. 10:12, 14)—No Sacraments
One Lord (1 Cor. 8:4; Eph. 4:5)—No Lawlessness

313   Three Thousand

The Law Given—3000 Slain (Exod. 32:28)
The Spirit Descends—3000 Saved (Acts 2:41)

At the descent of the Lawgiver, *Judgment* fell on the lawbreakers
At the descent of the Spirit, *Grace* came to Christ's murderers

314   Two Seekers

The Sinner seeking the Savior (Luke 19:2)
The Savior seeking the Sinner (Luke 19:10)

These great truths are the complement of each other

315   Three Golden Links

(John 5:24)

"Heareth" (Isa. 55:3; Rom. 10:17; Matt. 13:23)
"Believeth" (John 6:29; Rom. 10:9; John 20:31)
"Hath" (John 3:36; 1 John 5:13; 1 Thess. 1:5)

316   Man's Refusals of God's Grace

Began to make *excuse* (Luke 14:18)—Triflers
Go thy way for this time (Acts 24:25)—Procrastinators
Ye will *not come* to Me (John 5:40)—Neglecters
They say, *Depart* from us (Job. 21:14)—Despisers
I called, but ye *refused* (Prov. 1:29)—Rejecters

317   Christ, the Rock

Smitten to give life (Ps. 78:20; 1 Cor. 10:4)
Cleft to give Shelter (Exod. 33:22; Song 2:14)
Raised to give Shadow (Isa. 32:2; 2 Sam. 22:3)
Exalted to give Glory (2 Sam. 22:47; Exod. 33:21)

318   Gospel Receivers:

Their Present Blessings and Prospects

They are justified (Acts 13:39)—Through Christ
They are saved (Eph. 2:9)—By Christ
They have everlasting life (John 3:16)—In Christ
They look for glory (Titus 2:13)—With Christ

319   Gospel Rejecters:

Their Present Condition and Coming Doom

They are condemned already (John 3:18)—Judicially
They have no life (1 John 5:9)—Spiritually
They are under wrath (John 3:36)—Actually
They shall be damned (Matt. 16:26)—Eternally

320   Two Tremblers

Felix (Acts 24:25) who procrastinated and perished
The Jailer (Acts 16:29) who believed and was saved

321   Life-giver and Judge

(John 5:20-29)

The Son of God (v. 25)—The Life-giver
The Son of Man (v. 27)—The Judge

All must have to do with Christ as one or the other

322   Contrasts—1

Whitewashed (Matt. 23:27)—The Hypocrite
Washed White (Rev. 7:14)—The Believing Sinner

323   Contrasts—2

Self-Justification (Luke 16:15)—The Self-Righteous
     Pharisee
Divine Justification (Luke 18:14)—The Convicted Sinner

324   Contrasts—3

What shall I do? (Mark 10:17)—Rich Man's Question
What wilt thou? (Mark 10:51)—Beggar's Opportunity

The First was asked the Savior, by a rich man who did nothing
The Second was asked a beggar by the Lord, who gave everything
The one went away "sorrowful"; the other "glorifying God"

325   According To

According to His Mercy (Titus 3:5)—Is our Salvation
According to His Riches (Phil. 4:19)—Is our Supply
According to His Power (Col. 1:11)—Is our Strength

326   The Work of the Spirit of God

Born of the Spirit (John 3:8)
Sealed by the Spirit (Eph. 1:13)
Indwelt by the Spirit (1 Cor. 3:16)

327   At Caeserea Philippi

(Matthew 16)

A Good Confession (v. 17)—"Revealed by God"
A Divine Revelation (v. 17)—"Thou art the Christ"
A Sound Foundation (v. 18)—"On this Rock I will
     build"

328   Ransom

A Ransom Found (Job 23:24)—By God
A Ransom Given (1 Tim. 2:5, 6)—By Christ
A Ransom Refused (Job 36:18)—By Unbelievers

329   "We Know"

That the Son of God is come (1 John 5:20)
That we have passed from death to life (1 John 3:14)
That we have eternal life (1 John 5:13)
That we shall be like Him (1 John 3:2)
That we have a House in Heaven (2 Cor. 5:1)

330   The Lost

The lost blinded by Satan (2 Cor. 4:3)
The lost sought by Christ (Luke 19:10)
The lost found by Christ (Luke 15:6)
The lost damned in hell (John 17:12)

331   Shut In and Shut Out

Shut in (Gen. 7:16, with John 10:28)—For Salvation
Shut out (Matt. 25:10, with Luke 13:12)—For Damnation

332   A Birthday Carnival

(Mark 6:14-29)

Herod, weak, fickle, cowardly—Sin's Servant
Herodias, wicked, revengeful, murderous—Satan's Slave
Salome, immodest, indecent, unmerciful—Satan's Tool
John, faithful, holy, martyr—Jesus' Friend

> A saint's martyrdom, a harlot's triumph, a monarch's weakness

333   Things I Know

I know Whom I have believed (2 Tim. 1:12)
I know that my Redeemer liveth (Job 19:25)
I know, God is for me (Ps. 56:9)

334 Four Reigns

Death reigned (Rom. 5:14)—From Adam to Moses
Law reigned (Gal. 3:23, 24)—Moses to Christ
Grace reigns (Rom. 5:21)—In this age
Righteousness will reign (Isa. 32:1)—In Millennium

335 God, Our Help

"Thou hast destroyed thyself; but in Me is thine help"
(Hosea 13:9)

Past Helper—"Thou hast been my help" (Ps. 63:7)
Present Helper—"A very present help" (Ps. 46:1)
Future Helper—"The Lord will help me" (Isa. 50:9)

336 Living Water

For us as a Gift (John 4:10, with Rev. 22:17)
In us as a Well (John 4:14, with John 10:10)
From us in Rivers (John 7:38, with Gal. 3:5)

337 Results of Gospel Preaching in Acts

They were *pricked* in heart (2:37)—Awakening
They were *cut* to the heart (7:54)—Conviction
Many which heard *believed* (4:4)—Faith
Believed and *turned* to the Lord (11:31)—Conversion
Hearing, believed and were *baptized* (18:8)—Confession

338 Divine Love

The Father's Love (John 17:23)—As to the Son
The Son's Love (John 15:13)—No Greater
The Saint's Love (John 15:12)—As Christ's to them

339 Debtors

Debtors to God (Luke 7:41)—The Sinners
Debtors to Law (Gal. 5:3)—Transgressors
Debtors to Grace (Matt. 18:32)—As Forgiven
Debtors to Others (Rom. 1:14)—As Stewards

340   Faith, Its Nature and Blessing

The *Word* of Faith (Rom. 10:8)—Preacher's Message
Hearing of faith (Gal. 3:2)—Listener's responsibility
Obedience of faith (Rom. 16:26)—Principle of blessing
Righteousness of faith (Rom. 4:13)—New Standing
Joy of faith (Phil. 1:25)—The Believer's Portion

341   Atonement, Advocacy, Advent

Atonement of Christ (Heb. 9)—On the Cross
Advocacy of Christ (1 John 2:1)—In the Heavens
Advent of Christ (1 John 3:2)—To the Air

342   Warning, Winning, Watching

Warning them *from* Christ (Acts 20:31)—Preacher
Winning them *to* Christ (Prov. 11:30)—Soulwinner
Watching them *for* Christ (Heb. 13:17)—Shepherd

343   Death

In Hebrews 2
The Fear of Death (v. 15)—Was the Sinner's
The Power of Death (v. 14)—Was the Devil's
The Suffering of Death (v. 9)—Was the Savior's
Deliverance from Death (v. 15)—Is the Believer's

344   Attrition and Contrition

"I have sinned" (Matt. 27:4)—*Attrition*, followed by Damnation
"I have sinned" (Luke 15:21)—*Contrition*, leading to Salvation

There is plenty of *attrition* on earth and in hell, but genuine *contrition* is the work of the Spirit of God leading to conversion.

345   Three Jehovah Titles

The order is that in which Faith apprehends Christ

Jehovah—tsidkenu, "The Lord, our Righteousness" (Jer. 23:6)

Jehovah—shalom, "The Lord, our Peace" (Judg. 6:24)

Jehovah—nissi, "The Lord, our Banner" (Exod. 17:15)

346   Gospel Purity

God of pure eyes (Hab. 1:13)—The Necessity

Pure in their own eyes (Prov. 30:12)—Counterfeit

Purified in obeying the truth (1 Peter 1:22)—The Instrument

Purifying their hearts by faith (Acts 15:9)—The Means

Purify unto Himself a people (Titus 2:14)—The Object

Keep thyself pure (1 Tim. 5:22)—The Responsibility

347   Three Offices of Christ

Christ, our Passover (1 Cor. 5:7)—Sacrificed for us

Christ, our Advocate (1 John 2:1)—Living for us

Christ, our Hope (1 Tim. 1:1)—Coming for us

348   Life From, in, and to Christ

In Him is Life (John 1:3)—The Source

I give unto them eternal life (John 10:28)—The Gift

He that hath the Son hath life (1 John 5:9)—Possession

Christ who is our life (Col. 3:4)—The Security

We live unto Christ (2 Cor. 5:15)—The Object

349   What God Has Sent

God sent His Son (1 John 4:9)—Into the World

The Word of Salvation (Acts 13:26)—The Gospel

The Salvation of God (Acts 28:28)—To Sinners

His Spirit (1 Peter 1:12)—To Convict and Convert

The Servants of God (Acts 13:4)—To Preach

350 The Whole World

God loved the World (John 3:16)
Christ's death is for it (1 John 2:2)
Satan deceiveth it (Rev. 12:9)
Sinners seek to gain it (Mark 8:36)

351 Things Which Are of God

(Romans 1)

The Gospel of God (v. 1)—His Message
The Power of God (v. 16)—His Salvation
The Righteousness of God (v. 17)—His Character
The Wrath of God (v. 18)—His Judgment

352 Four Legal Questions

(Romans 8:31-35)

Who can be against us? (v. 31)—No Accuser
Who lay anything to our charge? (v. 33)—No Prosecutor
Who is he that condemneth? (v. 34)—No Judge
Who shall separate us? (v. 36)—No Jailer

353 None

There is none upright (Mic. 7:2)
There is none righteous (Rom. 3:10)
There is none good (Matt. 19:17)
There is none that seeketh God (Rom. 3:11)

354 The Salvation of God

(Acts 28:28)

A Great Salvation (Heb. 2:3)
A Present Salvation (2 Cor. 6:2)
A Common Salvation (Jude 3)
A Known Salvation (Luke 1:77)
An Eternal Salvation (Heb. 5:9)

355   Noah's Times and Testimony

Judgment Pronounced (Gen. 6:13, with Heb. 11:7)
Righteousness Preached (Gen. 6:22, with 2 Peter 2:5)
Longsuffering Prevailed (Gen. 6:3, with 1 Peter 3:20)
Salvation Prepared (Gen. 6:14, with 1 Peter 3:20)
The Spirit Persuading (Gen. 6:3, with 1 Peter 3:19)
Sinners Perished (Gen. 7:21, with 2 Peter 3:6)

356 Preaching Christ, and the Results

On Jerusalem's Streets (Acts 2:14, 42)—3000 Saved
At the Temple Gate (Acts 3:12; 4:4)—5000 Believed
In a Soldier's House (Acts 10:24, 44)—Household saved
In a Desert Chariot (Acts 8:30)—Rider Converted
At a Riverside (Acts 16:13)—Lydia's heart opened
In a Prison (Acts 16:31, 34)—Jailer Converted

357   The Touch of Jesus

Gives Life (Luke 7:14)—To the Dead
Gives Cleansing (Luke 5:12)—To the Vile
Gives Healing (Matt. 8:15)—To the Sin-sick
Gives Blessing (Mark 10:16)—To the Little Ones

358   What Christ Did, Does, and Will Do

He Died—Christ died for our sins (1 Cor. 15:3)
He Rose—Raised for our justification (Rom. 4:25)
He Lives—Lives to make intercession (Heb. 7:25)
He Comes—Coming to receive us (John 14:3)

359   Great Transitions

From Death to Life (John 5:24)
From Darkness to Light (1 Peter 2:9)
From Bondage to Liberty (Gal. 5:13)
From Satan to God (Acts 26:18)

360　　　　Paul's Testimonies

Paul's Conversion—"I obtained mercy" (1 Tim. 1:16)
Paul's Confession—"Sinners. . .I am chief" (1 Tim. 1:15)
Paul's Persuasion—"I am persuaded," etc. (Rom. 8:38)
Paul's Determination—"I determined," etc. (1 Cor. 2:2)

361　　　　Jehovah Revealed

In Psalm 103

As Redeemer (v. 4)—We are Slaves
As Healer (v. 3)—We are Sick
As Satisfier (v. 5)—We are Empty
As Father (v. 13)—We are Children
As Ruler (v. 19)—We are Subjects

362　　　　What Has Been Shed?

Christ's Blood shed *for* us (Matt. 26:28)
The Spirit shed *on* us (Titus 3:6)
God's Love shed *abroad* in us (Rom. 5:5)

363　　　　Two Great Facts

Christ died for us—Substitution (Rom. 5:6)
We died with Him—Identification (Rom. 6:6)

364　　The Work of God in the Soul

Begun at Conversion (Phil. 1:6)
Progresses through Life (Phil 2:12,13)
Completed at Christ's Coming (Phil. 3:21)

365　　　What the Gospel Ministers

(2 Corinthians 3:6-18)

Life (v. 6, with John 10:10)
The Spirit (v. 8, with Eph. 1:13)
Righteousness (v. 9, with Rom. 1:17)
Transformation to His Image (v. 18, with 1 John 3:2)

366   The Gospel Call

Called by the Gospel (2 Thess. 2:14)—The Instrument
Called by God's Grace (Gal. 1:15)—The Source
Called out of Darkness (1 Peter 2:9)—The Position
Called to Glory (2 Peter 1:3)—The Prospect

367   Some Old Time Preachers and Their Subjects

Enoch preached Judgment to Come (Jude 14)
Noah preached Righteousness (2 Peter 2:5)
Nathan preached Sin (2 Sam. 12:7)
Elijah preached Decision (1 Kings 18:21)
Micaiah preached Death (2 Chron. 18:21)
John preached Repentance (Matt. 3:2)
Peter preached Christ (Acts 4:11,12)

368   Salvation Is of the Lord

Salvation *belongeth* to the Lord (Ps. 3:8)—Its Origin
Salvation is *of* the Lord (Jonah 2:9)—Its Worker
Salvation is *by* the Lord (1 Thess. 5:9)—Its Giver
Salvation is *in* the Lord (2 Tim. 2:10)—Its Security

369   The Stone

A Foundation Stone (1 Peter 2:4; Isa. 28:16; 1 Cor. 3:11)—
     In Death
A Living Stone (1 Peter 2:5, 6)—In Resurrection
A Corner Stone (Eph. 2:19)—In Glory
A Crushing Stone (Dan. 2:45)—In Judgment

370   Christ, the Word

The Eternal Word (John 1:1)—In the Past
The Incarnate Word (John 1:14)—On Earth
The Exalted Word (Heb. 1:1)—In Heaven
The Avenging Word (Rev. 19:13)—In Judgment

371   Three Personal Blessings

A Personal Savior (Luke 1:47)—"My Savior"
A Present Salvation (2 Tim. 1:9)—"Hath Saved"
A Glorious Prospect (Phil. 3:20)—"We look for"

372   What God Provides for Himself

God provides a Lamb (Gen. 22:8)—To Die
God provides a King (1 Sam. 16:1)—To Rule
>   Both are fulfilled in Christ

373   Justification in Four Aspects

Justified by *Grace* (Rom. 3:24)—Intrinsically
Justified by *Blood* (Rom. 5:9)—Meritoriously
Justified by *Faith* (Rom. 5:1)—Instrumentally
Justified by *Works* (James 2:24)—Evidentially

374   The Wrath of God

By nature, sinners are children of wrath (Eph. 2:3)
By unbelief, sinners are subjects of wrath (John 3:36)
In eternity, sinners are endurers of wrath (Rev. 14:10,11)
In Christ, sinners are delivered from wrath (1 Thess. 1:10)

375   Sanctification

Sanctification by Blood (Heb. 13:12)—By the Cross
Sanctification by the Spirit (1 Peter 1:2)—At Conversion
Sanctification in the Truth (John 17:17)—Progressive

376   Twofold Redemption

Redemption by *Price* (1 Peter 1:19, with Exod. 13:13)
Redemption by *Power* (Exod. 6:6, with Ps. 49:15)

>   The former has its type in the Blood of the Paschal Lamb (Exod. 12);
> the latter in the deliverance at the Red Sea (Exod. 14)

377 Sin

Sin put away by Sacrifice (Heb. 9:26)
Forgiven in Grace (Eph. 1:7)
Blotted out in Righteousness (Isa. 44:22)
Remembered no more in Judgment (Heb. 10:17)

378 Work of the Spirit

Convicting the sinner (John 16:8)—General work
Regenerating the believer (John 3:5)—Special work
Sealing the saint (Eph. 1:13)—His abiding work

379 The Love of God, in Four Stages

Manifested (1 John 4:9)—In the Sending of His Son
Commended (Rom. 5:8)—In the Death of Christ
Believed (1 John 4:16)—As set forth in the Gospel
Experienced (Rom. 5:5)—Shed abroad in the heart

The first two are objective, something to look away to. Believed, it becomes a subjective power in the saint.

380 Threefold Rest

Rest for the Sinner (Matt. 11:28)—In Christ's Work
Rest for the Saint (Matt. 11:29)—Under Christ's Yoke
Rest for the Servant (Mark 6:30)—In His Presence

381 First Questions, in the Old and the New Testament

Where art thou? (Gen. 3:1-9)—God seeking the sinner
Where is He? (Matt. 2:2)—Man seeking the Savior

382 Divine Life in Three Stages

Translated at Conversion (Col. 1:13)
Transformed by Contemplation (2 Cor. 3:18)
Transfigured in Consummation (1 John 3:2)

383 Candles

Candle of Conscience (Prov. 20:27)—Natural Man
Candle of Conviction (Luke 15:8)—Spirit and Word
Candle of Life (Matt. 5:15)—The New Birth
Candle of Testimony (Luke 11:36)—Life Manifested

384 The New Birth

Its Necessity (John 3:3, 5)
Its Nature (Gal. 6:15, with 2 Cor. 5:17)
How Effected (1 John 5:1, with 1 Peter 1:23)
How Manifested (1 John 3:8-10; 5:24)

385 Forgiveness of Sins

Promised by Christ (Matt. 12:31)
Procured at the Cross (Eph. 1:7)
Proclaimed in the Gospel (Acts 13:38)
Received by Faith (Acts 26:18)
Known to the Believer (1 John 2:12)

386 Eternal Life

The Sinner has it not (John 6:53; Eph. 2:1)
God is the Giver of it (Rom. 6:23)
Christ is the Imparter of it (John 10:28)
Faith Receives it (John 3:15, 36)
The Believer Possesses it (1 John 5:13)
The Unbeliever Rejects it (John 5:40)

387 The Blood

Atones for Sin (Lev. 17:2)
Shelters from Wrath (Exod. 12:13)
Redeems to God (1 Peter 1:19)
Makes Peace (Col. 1:20)
Looses from Sin (Rev. 1:5)
Brings nigh to God (Eph 2:13)
Gives the Victory (Rev. 12:11)

388   Judgment

It follows Death (Heb. 9:27)
The Day is Appointed (Acts 17:31)
The Scene Described (Rev. 20:11)
Christ Sustained it for His people (Isa. 53:5)
The Believer cometh not into it (John 5:24)

389   Conversion

Its Necessity (Matt. 18:3; Acts 3:19)
The Reason Why (Isa. 53:6; Ps. 119:176)
How Produced (Acts 26:18; 1 Thess. 2:9)
Its Manifestation (1 Thess. 1:10; 1 Peter 2:25)
Hindrances (Acts 28:27)

390   Disciples

The Gospel's Object (Matt. 28:18)
The Apostle's Practice (Acts 14:21)
The Disciple's Badge (John 13:35)
The Disciple's Path (Luke 14:26)

391   Salvation and Service

No unsaved one can please God (Rom. 8:8)
No worldly one can serve Christ (Matt. 6:24)
Jesus served and suffered for us (Matt. 20:28)
He wrought and finished it (John 17:4)
Saved apart from works (Eph. 2:9)
Saved to serve (1 Thess. 1:9)

392   Means

God will by *no means* clear the guilty (Exod. 34:7)
None can by *any means* redeem his brother (Ps. 49:7)
Gospellers seek by *all means* to save some (1 Cor. 9:22)
Sinner can by *no means* escape from hell (Matt. 5:26)

393 Bundles

Bundle of the Yoke (Isa. 58:6, margin)—Sin
Bundle of Life (1 Sam. 25:29)—Salvation
Bundle of Myrrh (Song 1:13)—Communion
Bundle of Tares (Matt. 13:30)—Judgment

394 Three Stages of the Christian Life

Believe in Me (John 14:1)—Life Received
Abide in Me (John 15:4)—Fruitfulness Ensured
Follow thou Me (John 21:22)—Progress Maintained

395 Excepts

The Sinner's Except (John 3:3)—Regeneration
The Savior's Except (John 12:24)—Atonement
The Saint's Except (John 15:4)—Fruitfulness

396 Three Periods

(Acts 17:30, 31)

The Past—Ignorance Overlooked
The Present—Repentance Commanded
The Future—Judgment Appointed

397 Love Manifested, Commended, Bestowed

Love Manifested (1 John 4:9)—In Christ's Life
Love Commended (Rom. 5:8)—By Christ's Death
Love Bestowed (1 John 3:1)—In Christ Risen

398 Christ Crucified

Proof of Man's Sin (Acts 2:23)
Fruit of God's Grace (Heb 2:9)
Cause of the Gospel's Power (1 Cor. 1:18, 22)

399   Everlasting Things

Everlasting Love (Jer. 31:3)—God's Love for Man
Everlasting Salvation (Isa. 45:17)—God's Gift to Man
Everlasting Destruction (2 Thess. 1:9)—Sin's Doom
Everlasting Fire (Matt. 25:46)—Sin's Punishment

400   Divine Wrath

Wrath Predicted for the Sinner (Job 20:23)
Wrath Endured by the Savior (Ps. 88:7)
Wrath Warned of by the Preacher (Matt. 3:7)
Wrath Escaped by the Believer (1 Thess. 1:10)

401   Brought Forth

Brought Forth to Death (John 19:13)—The Savior
Brought to Life (John 11:44)—Christ Receiver
Brought From Bondage (Deut. 26:8)—Redeemed
Brought Forth to Wrath (Job 21:30)—The Christless

402   Three Grand Realities

In Ephesians 1

Chosen by God (v. 4)—The Eternal Purpose
Redeemed by Christ (v. 7)—The Procuring Cause
Sealed by the Spirit (v. 13)—The Preserving Power

403   Saved, Sealed, Shown

(Ephesians 2:5-7)

Saved by Grace (v. 5)—The Principle
Seated in Christ (v. 6)—The Place
Shown in Glory (v. 7)—The Prospect

404   Ready for Heaven or Hell

Heaven prepared for the Believer (1 Peter 1:4)
The Believer prepared for Heaven (Col. 1:12)
Hell awaiting the Sinner (Matt. 25:46)
The Sinner already fitted to be there (Rom. 9:22)

OUTLINES ON BIBLE QUESTIONS

405   **2 Samuel 19:34**

"How long have I to live?"

Answer—Job 14:1; 1 Sam. 20:3; Prov. 27:1

406   **Job 21:7**

"Wherefore do the wicked live?"

Answer—Ezek. 33:11; 2 Peter 3:9; 1 Tim. 2:4

407   **Zechariah 1:5**

"Your fathers, where are they?"

Answer—Saved (Phil 1:23; 2 Cor. 5:8)
Unsaved (Luke 16:23; Rev. 20:13)

408   **Genesis 3:9**

"Where art thou?"

Answer—Isa. 59:2; Eph. 2:12, 13; Isa. 53:6

409   **1 Kings 18:21**

"How long halt ye?"

Answer—2 Cor. 6:2; Heb. 3:7; Prov. 27:1; Gen. 19:17

410   **Job 14:10**

"Man giveth up the ghost, and where is he?"

Answer—If saved, with Christ (Acts 7:59; Phil. 1:23; Luke
23:43)

If unsaved, in Hell (Luke 16:23; Ps. 9:17; Rev.
20:13)

411   **Job 25:3**

"How can man be justified with God?"

Answer—Not by works (Rom. 3:20)

By Grace alone (Rom. 3:24; Titus 3:7)

Through Faith (Rom. 5:1; Gal. 2:16)

412   **Job 14:14**

"If a man die, shall he live again?"

Answer—Job 19:25; 1 Cor. 25:22, 23; John 5:28

413   **Genesis 24:58**

"Wilt thou go with this man?"

Two Answers—Gen. 29:29; Num. 10:30

414   **Jeremiah 13:21**

"What wilt thou say when He shall punish thee?"

Answer—Matt. 22:12; 1 Sam. 2:9

415   **Luke 13:23**

"Are there few that be saved?"

Answer—John 10:9; Acts 16:31; Rom. 10:9

416   **Hebrews 2:3**

"How shall we escape if we neglect so great
salvation?"

Answer—Heb. 12:25; 1 Thess. 5:3

417   Mark 10:26

"Who then can be saved?"

Answer—1 Tim. 1:15; John 10:9; Acts 16:31; 1 Tim. 2:4

418   Matthew 22:42

"What think ye of Christ?"

Various Estimates (Matt. 16:13-15)
The Jews (Isa. 53:2, 3)
The World (John 7:12)
The Believer (Matt. 16:13-16)
The Bride (Song 4:16)

419   Isaiah 33:14

"Who among us shall dwell with the devouring fire?"

Answer—Rev. 20:15; Jude 7; Heb. 6:7

420   Isaiah 33:14

"Who among us shall lie down with everlasting
burnings?"

Answer—Matt. 25:41,46; 2 Thess. 1:9; Rev. 21:8

421   Jeremiah 3:19

"How shall I put thee among the children?"

Answer—John 3:5; John 1:12; 1 John 3:1

422   Job 14:4

"Who can bring a clean thing out of an unclean?"

Answer—God (Isa. 51:10; 1 John 1:7; John 15:3)

423   1 Samuel 30:13

"To whom belongest thou?"

Answer—Matt. 6:24; Acts 27:23; John 8:44

424   Matthew 23:33

"How can ye escape the damnation of hell?"

Answer—Ps. 66:13; 1 Thess. 1:10; Rom. 8:1

425   Is There a Hell?

The Lord Jesus warns of it (Mark 9:43-45)

The Lord Jesus unveils it (Luke 16:23-28)

The Word of God describes it (Jude 7; 2 Peter 2:17)

426   Do Men Exist Forever?

Yes; in Eternal Glory or Eternal Woe

There is no Annihilation (John 3:36; Matt. 25:46)

There is no Restitution (Mark 3:29; Matt. 12:31, 32)

The State of All is Eternal (Rev. 22:11)

427   Is the Bible God's Word?

It claims to be so itself (2 Tim. 3:16; Prov. 30:5)

Christ acknowledged it (Luke 24:27; Mark 7:13)

The Apostles owned it so (2 Peter 1:20, 21; 3:16)

428   Does Death End All?

For the Beasts, it does; for Man, it does not

Man has the Breath of God (Gen. 2:7; Eccl. 3:21)

The Lord spoke of existence beyond (Matt. 10:28)

The Word confirms it (Matt. 22:32)

429   Is There a God?

The Fool says—No (Ps. 14:1)

The Agnostic says—He is unknown (Acts 17:23)

The sinner desires not to know (Job 21:14)

God is known in His works (Ps. 19:1; Rom. 1:19)

God is manifested in His Son (John 1:18; 1 John 4:9)

God is known by His People (John 17:3; Col. 1:10

430   Does the Soul Sleep?

No. Only the body (Acts 7:60; 1 Thess. 4:13)
After Death (Phil. 1:23; 2 Cor. 5:6; Luke 16:21-24)
After Resurrection (1 Cor. 15:52-54; John 5:28,29)

431   Will All Men Be Saved?

The Lord says—No (Matt. 7:13, 14)
The Spirit says—No (Phil. 3:19; 2 Thess. 2:12; Heb. 6:8)
    Examples—2 Peter 2:6; Jude 7; Rev. 21:8

432   Is There Probation After Death?

Answer—Luke 16:22-31; Heb. 9:27; John 5:28, 29

433   Can We Be Sure of Salvation in This Life?

Believers *are* Saved (1 Cor. 15:2; 2 Tim. 1:9)
Believers *have* Eternal Life (John 3:36; 1 John 5:9)
Believers *know* it (1 John 5:13; 3:16; 2 Cor. 5:1)

OUTLINES ON TYPES

434   Aprons and Coats

(Genesis 3:7-21)

Four Conditions in which Adam and Eve are found

1. Innocent (Gen. 1:2, with Eccl. 7:20)—in God's image, liable to fall
2. Fallen (Gen. 3:7, with Rom. 5:12)—so all his seed (Eph. 2:2)
3. Clad in Fig-leaves (Gen. 3:7, with Rom. 10:3; Luke 16:15)—Self-righteousness
4. Clothed in Coats of Skin (Gen. 3:21)—Righteousness founded on Redemption (2 Cor. 5:21; Phil. 3:3)

435   Cain and Abel

(Genesis 4:1-16; Hebrews 11:4; Jude 11)

In what they were alike; in what they differed

Both Sons of Fallen Adam (Gen. 5:3; Rom. 5:19; Ps. 51:5)
Both were Offerers, both acknowledged God (Luke 18:10-14)

Cain: Self-righteous, offers fruit; no sin acknowledged; no blood, no faith; disowned by God; works evil (1 John 3:12), hates and kills his brother; lies to God, despises grace, flees from Him, seeks to forget guilt, makes himself happy without God

Abel: Owns fall, brings offering; type of Christ, sheds blood in faith; God accepts; he is counted righteous (Heb. 11:4), "Righteous Abel" (Matt. 23:33); then suffers on earth, and, dying a martyr, goes to heaven

436 Noah and the Ark

(Genesis 6, 7, 8)

Man's Iniquity (*cf.* Gen. 6:5 with 1:31; Ps. 14:2)

Judgment pronounced (Gen. 6:13, 17, with Luke 17:26)

Noah Warned (Heb. 11:7; 2 Peter 3:5-10)

Ark Provided—Christ. Pitch, Ransom, the Cross

Noah Invited (Gen. 7:1)—"Come"; obeyed, shut in, the world shut out, secure (John 10:28)

Window, light, communion (Ps. 5:3)—food (John 6:57; Jer. 15:16)

Ararat (Gen. 8:4)—Resurrection, new creation (Eph. 2:6)

Raven and Dove (Gen. 8:7, 8)—two natures (Gal. 5:17; Rom. 13:14)

Go Forth (Gen. 8:16)—nothing lost, all saved, worship, purged earth, rainbow

437 Abram Justified

(Genesis 15:1-18; Romans 4:1-4, 20-23; James 2:23,24)

The Promise of God (Gen. 15:5), sure; so Rom. 4:24, 5:1

Faith takes God at His Word (Rom. 4:3, 20; John 3:33)

Counted Righteous Godward (2 Cor. 5:21; Rom. 4:5)

Works, the Proof of Faith, Manward (James 2:21-23)

438 Sodom's Destruction

(Genesis 19:1-30; Luke 17:28-32)

Three Classes appear, representative of Sinners now

The Sodomites (Gen. 19:24), in the City—Careless Sinners

Lot's Wife (Gen. 19:26), on the Plain—Halting Sinners

Lot and his Daughters (Gen. 19:30), in Zoar—Saved Sinners

> The first were utterly godless, "sinners exceedingly"
> The second was the wife of a just man, yet unsaved
> The third were warned, lingered, yet saved as by fire

439 Rebekah; or, the Call of the Bride

(Genesis 24)

Father, Son, and Servant in Hebron (Gen. 24:1-4)—Trinity in Counsel

The Son, Dead and Risen (Gen. 22)—Christ in Heaven waiting (Acts 2:24, 33)

Servant sent forth—Holy Spirit with Gospel (1 Peter 1:12; Acts 2:1-3)

To call, win, and bring home a Bride for His Son (Acts 15:14; 2 Cor. 11:2)

The Servant's Testimony to (Gen. 24:36-43) and Gifts from the Son (Gen. 24:53; John 3:35, 36)

Decision, Separation, and Pilgrimage of the Bride (Gen. 24:58-61; Phil. 3:7, 8; Ps. 45:10; John 14:3)

Seeing and Meeting with Issac (1 John 3:2; 1 Thess. 4:17); Presentation and Union (Rev. 19:7; 21:2)

440 Joseph and His Brethren

(Genesis 37, 39, 41, 42, 45)

Joseph is a Type of Christ in suffering and glory

Beloved of his Father (Gen. 37:3, with John 3:35; Matt. 3:17)

Hated by his Brethren (Gen. 37:4, with John 8:40; 15:23; Luke 23:2)

Rejected and Sold (Gen. 37:28, with Matt. 26:14; 27:28; Amos 6:6)

Numbered with Transgressors (Gen. 39:20, with Mark 15:28; Luke 23:39-41)

Exaltation and Glory (Gen. 41:43, with Phil. 2:9,10; Eph. 1:20)

"Go to Joseph" (Gen. 41:55, with Col. 1:19; 2:9; John 6:37)

Need and Conviction (Gen. 42:11, 21, with Job 27:6; v. 21, with Job 41:4)

Reconciliation and Blessing (Gen. 45:4, 5, with Luke 7:42; 15:20)

441   Seven "I wills"

(Exodus 6:6-8)

These embrace the whole work of Redemption

"I will bring you out," with Gal. 1:4

"I will rid you out of bondage," John 8:32-36

"I will redeem you," Titus 2:14

"I will take you to me for a people," 1 Peter 2:9,10

"I will be to you a God," 2 Cor. 6:16

"I will bring you unto the land," John 17:24

"I will give it you for an heritage," 1 Peter 1:3-5

442   The Red Sea

(Exodus 14:1-3, 13-31)

The Death of Christ, delivering from the world and Satan

The Trembling Host; not knowing deliverance, as Gal. 1:4; Col. 1:13

The Strong Enemy; Satan, Prince (John 12:21), and power (Acts 26:18)

The Opened Sea; Death abolished (2 Tim. 1:10; Heb. 2:14)

The Walk of Faith (Heb. 11:29; 1 Thess. 5:9, 10)

443   The Salvation of the Lord

(Exodus 14:13,31; 15:1)

Salvation Wrought out by Jehovah (Exod. 14:13,21; Heb. 5:9)

Salvation Appropriated by Faith (Exod. 14:22,29; Isa. 12:2)

Salvation Enjoyed in Praise (Exod. 15:1; 14:31; Ps. 40:3)

444   The Manna

(Exodus 16:1-11; Numbers 11:6; 21:5)

Hungry People, the world, hungry, unsatisfied (Isa. 55:2)

Free Gift of God, Christ (John 6:51; Ps. 105:40)

White & Sweet, Christ (Song 5:16); Word (Ps. 119:140)

Gathered & Eaten, Faith's Appropriation (2 Tim. 1:12)

Neglected, Rejected, Loathed (Heb. 2:3; John 12:48)

445   ## The Passover

(Exodus 11:5; 12)

I.—God's Judgment

Judgment Pronounced (Exod. 11:5, 6; 12:12)

Long Delayed (Gen. 15:16, with 2 Peter 3:9; Eccl. 8:11)

Quickly Executed (Exod. 12:29, with 1 Thess. 5:2; 2 Peter 3:10)

II.—The Redeemer and the Redeemed

Redemption Announced (Exod. 11:7; 12:3)

The Redeemer; the lamb, character, manner, and time of death

The Redeemed, new born (Exod. 12:2); within (Exod. 12:22); feeding (Exod. 12:8); girded (Exod. 12:11)

The Redemption, safety (Exod. 12:13); separation (Exod. 12:42)

III.—The Lamb

The Lamb Chosen (Exod. 12:5; 1 Peter 1:20)—In Eternal Past

The Lamb Kept (Exod. 12:5; Matt. 3:17; 17:5)—Christ in Life

The Lamb Slain (Exod. 12:6; 1 Cor. 5:7)—Christ Sacrificed

The Lamb Roasted (Exod. 12:8; Ps. 88:7; 89:46)—A Suffering Christ

The Lamb Fed On (Exod. 12:5, 8; 1 Cor. 5:8)—Communion

IV.—The Blood

The Blood Shed (Exod. 12:6; 1 Peter 1:19)—Atonement

The Blood Preserved (Exod. 12:22; Rom. 3:25)—Propitiation

The Blood Sprinkled by man (Exod. 12:7)—Appropriation

The Blood Seen by Jehovah (Exod. 12:13)—Satisfaction

V.—Safety, Assurance, Peace

The Blood made Safe (Exod. 12:13, with Heb. 11:28)

Word made Sure (Exod. 12:23; Rom. 3:4; 1 John 5:10)

Faith brought Peace (Exod. 12:28, with Col. 1:20; Rom. 5:1)

446   The Smitten Rock

(Exodus 17:1-7; Psalm 114:8)

"That Rock was Christ" (1 Cor. 10:4)

The Thirsty Host, sinners in the world (Isa. 55:1; John 4:14)

The Smitten Rock, Christ in death (Isa. 53:4); to give life (John 10:10)

The Flowing Stream, Life from Christ (John 7:36; Rev. 22:17)

The Thirsty Satisfied, never thirst (John 4:14); dispensing to others (John 7:38)

447   Balaam's Prayer, Prophecy, and Doom

(Numbers 23:7-24)

A Covetous Man (2 Peter 2:15-22; Jude 11)

A Religious Professor (Titus 1:16; Rev. 2:14)

Confession (22:34); "I have sinned," not repentance

Prayer (v. 10), "Let me die" (Eccl. 11:3; Gal. 6:7)

Despises God's Priest (v. 3), 2 Peter 2:1; Jude 12, 13

His Choice (24:17), "not now" (Acts 24:25), "not nigh" (Luke 16:26)

His End (Num. 31:8; Josh. 13:23)

448   The Leper

(Leviticus 13:1-18)

Leprosy: type of sin in the flesh; fallen man
Leper: a sinner unclean by nature, by practice defiled

His State, "utterly unclean" (Isa. 1:6; Rom. 3:9)

His Place, "without the camp"; afar off (Eph. 2:12)

His Confession, "Unclean" (Job 40:4; Isa. 6:5)

His Doom (Rev. 21:27; 22:11)

Sin separates from God, severs from saints, shuts out of heaven

449   The Leper's Cleansing

(Leviticus 14:1-18)

The Priest "shall go forth"—God's representative moves first (John 3:17; 1 Tim. 1:15)

The Sacrifice, "alive and clean"—Christ in life and holiness, slain

Cedar, Scarlet, Hyssop—Nature in greatness, glory, weakness

Living Bird Let Loose—Christ in Resurrection (Rom. 4:25)

Water Sprinkled—The Word, the Gospel (1 Peter 1:25; 1 Thess. 1:5)

Clean and Cleansing (John 15:3; 2 Cor. 7:2; Col. 3:8)

Sanctified and Anointed (1 Cor. 6:20; 1 John 2:27)

450   The Atonement

(Leviticus 16:1-19; Hebrews 9:22-28)

The Two Goats, Christ's Death, Godward and Manward

The Lord's Lot, Christ's Atonement, Godward (Heb. 9:14; Eph. 5:2)

Slain, Sprinkled, Propitiation (Rom. 3:25; 1 John 2:5)

Scapegoat, Christ the Sinbearer (1 Peter 2:24; Isa. 53:6)

Rest to People (v. 31), work death (23:30; Rom. 4:4)

451   The Year of Jubilee

(Leviticus 25:1-28)

The Inheritance Lost (Lam. 5:2; Gen. 3:24)

Owner a Slave (Rom. 7:14; John 8:34; Rom. 6:20)

Unable to Redeem (Ps. 49:7; Luke 7:42)

Redemption by Blood (Lev. 25:9; Eph. 1:7; Rom. 6:22)

Proclamation of Liberty (Luke 4:18; Acts 26:17)

Restoration of Inheritance (Heb. 9:15; 1 Peter 1:4)

452 The Brazen Serpent
(Numbers 21:1-9; John 3:14)

Dying People—The world, lawless, godless, under sin
Confession, "We have sinned"—Awakening, conviction
The Remedy—Man sinned: Man, Christ Jesus dies
The Life-look—From self to Christ (Isa. 45:22)
Cross without Christ—Can't save (see 2 Kings 18:4)

453 Korah's Sin and Doom
(Numbers 16:1-35; Jude 11)

Lawless and Rebellious (Num. 16:2, with 2 Peter 2:2, 10)
Despise God's Prophet and Priest (Num. 16:3, with 2 Peter 2:1; Jude 12, 13)
Exalt themselves (Num. 16:10; 2 Thess. 2:4; 1 John 2:19)
Brought to Judgment (Num. 16:16; 2 Thess. 2:8-10; Jude 15)
Sent alive into the pit (Rev. 19:20; 20:10)

454 The Sons of Korah
(Numbers 16:22, 33, with 26:11)

Father's house overwhelmed in judgment (Jude 11)
Sons saved by Grace (Eph. 2:9; Ps. 86:13)
Fellow-citizens of Priests (1 Chron. 6:31-35; Eph. 2:19)
Lodging around the Temple (1 Chron. 9:27; Ps. 91:1)
Leaders of Praise (see Psalms 42-44, headings)
Serve God day and night (1 Chron. 9:33; Rev. 7:15)

455 The Cities of Refuge
(Joshua 20:1-9)

The Manslayer's Danger (Matt. 3:7; Mark 3:29)
The Avenger's Power (Job 37:17; Rom. 6:23)
The Place of Safety, provided by God (Heb. 6:18)
The One Way (Deut. 19:3; John 14:6; Acts 16:17)
Open Gate and Welcome (Josh. 20:4; Luke 15:3; John 6:37)
Safe while Priest lives (Josh. 20:5,6; John 10:28; Heb. 7:25)

456   Names of the Cities of Refuge

(Joshua 20:7-9)
Expressing the Believer's Place and Portion in Christ

Kadesh, "Holy," Christ's Person (Luke 1:35; Acts 4:27)
Shechem, "Shoulder," Christ's Power (Luke 15:5)
Hebron, "Fellowship," Believer's Privilege (1 John 1:3)
Bezer, "Stronghold," Believer's Portion (1 Peter 1:4)
Ramoth, "Exalted," Believer's Place (Eph. 2:6)
Golan, "Happy," Believer's Condition (Phil. 4:1)

457   Rahab's Faith

(Joshua 2:1-22; 6:17-25; Hebrews 11:31)

Condemned City (Josh. 6:1; John 12:31; Rom. 3:19)
Abandoned Sinner (Josh. 2:2; Matt. 21:31, 32; 1 Tim. 1:15)
Believed God's Word (Josh 2:9,10; Rom. 3:4)
Receives Messengers (Josh 2:4; Heb. 11:31; Mark 9:37)
Binds Scarlet Thread (Josh 2:18; Exod. 12:13; Eph. 1:7)
Accepts Testimony (Josh 2:21; John 3:33; Rom. 10:17)
Is Saved and Exalted (Josh. 6:6, 23, 35; Matt. 1:5)

458   Naaman the Leper

(2 Kings 5:1-18)

Worldly Greatness and Fame (v. 1; Eccl. 2:11, 17)
A Leper (v. 1); Sin in Nature (Rom. 5:12; Isa. 1:6)
Hears of a Remedy (v. 4)
Starts to wrong place, in wrong way (v. 5; Rom. 3:17)
God's Prophet (v. 9); Christ in grace (Rom. 5:23)
Clear Message (v. 10; 1 John 1:7; Rev. 1:5)
Pride, Anger (vv. 11, 12); Man's Thoughts (Isa. 55:8, 9)
Humiliation, Cleansing (vv. 13,14; John 3:3; 2 Cor. 5:17)
Confession, Conversion (vv. 15,17; Rom. 10:9; Luke 17:17)

459   The Captive, Captain, and Covetous Servant

(2 Kings 5)

The Little Captive Maid (v. 2)—A True Witness
Channel of Blessing (vv. 3,4)—Honored Testimony
The Great Man Cleansed (vv. 14-19)—Great Result
Covetous Servant (v. 20)—A Hypocrite Unmasked
The Liar and his Doom (vv. 22, 37)—Divine Judgment

460   Joshua, the High Priest

From Filthy Garments to a Fair Mitre (Crown)
(Zechariah 3:1-8)

Stripped (v. 4, with Isa. 64:6; Job 27:6)
Cleansed (v. 4, with Heb. 1:3; Rev. 1:5)
Clothed (v. 5, with Luke 15:22; Phil. 3:9)
Crowned (v. 5, with Ps. 103:4; 1 Peter 2:9)

461 Isaiah's Conviction and Conversion

(Isaiah 6:1-8)

Conviction of State (v. 4; Job 42:5, 6)
Confession of Sin (v. 5; Ps. 51:4, 5)
Cleansing by Sacrifice (v. 7; Heb. 10:17-22)
Commission to Serve (v. 8; Heb. 9:14; 1 Thess. 1:9)

462   Jonah's Voyage

(Jonah 1, 2)

A Runaway from God (1:3)—The Sinner (Gen. 4)
A Rude Awakening (1:6)—Arrested (Acts 16:29)
Conviction (2:2-6)—Needful Experience (Ps. 116:1)
Vows and Prayer (2:7)—No Deliverance (Titus 3:5)
Salvation of the Lord (2:9)—End of Effort (Titus 2:11)
Deliverance (2:10)—Salvation Known (Ps. 40:2)

463   Moriah

The Place of Sacrifice Offered (Gen. 22)
The Place of Judgment Stayed (2 Sam. 24)
The Place of Worship Ascending (2 Chron. 3)

The Cross is the answer to the whole
There the Substitute was offered and accepted (Rom. 5:6; Eph. 5:2)
There Judgment was executed (Zech. 13:7; John 5:24)
There the Church is built, and worship ascends (Matt. 16:18; Heb. 13:15)

OUTLINES ON BIBLE TEXTS

464   Fourfold Prayer of Psalm 28:9

Answered in Christ

"Save Thy People" (with Matt. 1:21)—The Savior
"Bless Thine Inheritance" (with Eph. 1:3)—The Owner
"Feed them also" (with Isa. 40:11)—The Shepherd
"Lift them up forever" (1 Thess. 4:13)—The Hope

465   A Grand Confession

(Isaiah 12:2)

"God," a Divine Person—The Source
"Is," a Definite Knowledge—The Certainty
"My," a Personal Possession—The Individuality
"Salvation," a Great Fact—The Reality

466   Fourfold Blessing

In Isaiah 33:16

Position—"Dwell on High," with Eph. 2:6
Protection—"Place of Defense," with Eph. 6:10
Provision—"Bread shall be given," with Phil. 4:19
Prospect—"Thine eyes shall see the King," with 1 John 3:2

467 Sinner's Fear; Saint's Prospect

(Isaiah 33:14-17)

The Sinner's Fear—"Sinners in Zion are afraid"
Hypocrite's Surprise—"Fearfulness for the hypocrites"
Christ-rejecter's Doom—"Dwell with devouring fire"
The Believer's Place—"He shall dwell on high"
The Saint's Prospect—"Thine eyes shall see the King"

468 Man's Guilt and God's Grace

(Isaiah 43:22-28)

God Forgotten (v. 22)—"Thou hast been weary of Me"
Man's Guilt (v. 23)—"Made to serve with thy sins"
Sovereign Grace (v. 25)—"For Mine own sake"
Complete Forgiveness—"Blotteth out . . . will not remember thy sins"

469 The Best-known Bible Text:

John 3:16

"For God"—Eternal Lover
"So Loved"—Unmeasurable Love
"The World that He Gave"—Unworthy Object
"His Only Begotten Son"—Greatest Gift
"That whosoever"—Largest Invitation
"Believeth in Him"—Simplest Way
"Should not Perish"—Mightiest Rescue
"But have Everlasting Life"—Richest Possession

470 The Mightiest Work

(1 Timothy 1:15)

"This is a faithful saying"—A Sure Declaration
Worthy of all acceptance"—A Safe Investment
"Christ Jesus came"—A Divine Mission
"Into the World"—A Needy Place
"To Save Sinners"—A Great Work
"I am Chief"—A Personal Confession

OUTLINES FOR
SPECIAL OCCASIONS

471   **Seaside Sermons**
The Sea and Its Wonders
The Troubled Sea (Isa. 57:20)—The Sinner's Sorrow
Waves and Billows (Ps. 42:7)—Savior's Sufferings
A Great Calm (Matt. 8:36)—Peace Made
Sunk in the Depths—(Mic. 7:19)—Sins Forgiven
No more Sea (Rev. 21:1)—Eternal Glory

472   **Sand and Rock**
(Matthew 7:24-27)
Two Foundations—Self and Christ
Two Builders—Sinner and Saint
Two Houses—Profession and Possession
Two Ends—Destruction and Glorification

473   **An Open-Air Address**
(Proverbs 1:20-27)
The Preacher (v. 20)—Wisdom, Christ (1 Cor. 1:30)
The Pulpit (v. 21)—Streets, Gates, Chief Places
Congregation (v. 22)—Simple Ones, Scorners, Fools
The Message (v. 23)—A Call, a Promise, a Declaration
The Result (vv. 24-27)—Hearers, Refusers, Despisers

474   The Voyage of Life

A Safe Boat (John 6:21)—Christ's Salvation
A Good Anchor (Heb. 6:19)—Hope fixed on Christ
The Other Side (Luke 8:22)—Glory to Come

475   A Sermon on Board Ship

A Ship of Salvation (Gen. 7:1)
A Good Captain (Heb. 2:10)
A Saved Crew (Acts 27:24)
A Good Passage (Ps. 23:6)
A Calm Haven (Ps. 107:30)

476   A Cottage Meeting Address

A Thread in the *Window* (Josh. 2:21)—For Salvation
A Writing on the *Gate* (Deut. 11:20)—For Guidance
A Window in the *Roof* (Gen. 6:16)—For Communion
A Light in the *House* (Luke 11:33)—For Testimony

477   A Court Sermon

(Acts 24:24-27)

The Preacher—Paul the Prisoner
The Hearers—Felix and Drusilla
The Subjects—Righteousness, temperance, judgment
The Effect—Felix Trembled
The Result—Go thy way

478   A Word to Harvesters

A Harvest Field of Olden Time (Ruth 2)

Boaz, owner and master (v. 1)—Christ, the Kinsman
Servant, set over reapers (v. 6)—The Holy Spirit
Gleaner, Gentile, widow—Sinner Saved, Satisfied
Harvesters (v. 7; John 4:38)—Servants of Christ

479   A Harvest Address

Fading Flowers (Isa. 28:1)—The Shortness of Life
Falling Leaves (Isa. 34:4)—Certainty of Death
Golden Grain (Mark 4:29)—The Fruit of Grace
Busy Reapers (John 4:38)—The Coming of Glory

480   Harvest Past

Spring, Seed-sowing (2 Tim. 3:15)—Youth's Instructor
Summer, Privilege (Luke 19:42)—Gospel Proclamation
Harvest, Ingathering (Jer. 8:20)—Seasons of Blessing
Winter, Storm (Matt. 7:25)—Judgment

481   Winter Scenes

Stormy Winds (Ps. 148:8)—Rough Awakening
A Snowy Day (1 Chron. 11:22)—Great Deliverance
Melted Ice (Ps. 147:18)—True Conversion
Showers of Hail (Isa. 28:17)—Coming Judgment

482   A Pottery Address

The Potter and His Vessel (Jeremiah 23:1-12)

The Worker—God (see Gen. 1:26,31)
Vessel Made—Man Created in God's Image (Eccl. 7:29)
Vessel Marred—Man Ruined (Rom. 1:28-30; Titus 3:3)
The Vessel Made Anew—Regeneration (2 Cor. 5:17;
    Eph. 2:10; Col. 3:10)

FUNERAL OUTLINES

483   The Gate and Goal

Death to Life (John 5:24)—Conversion
Departure to be with Christ (Phil. 1:23)—Consolation
Waiting to be like Christ (1 John 3:1)—Consummation

484   "Resurgum"

Resurrection of Christ (1 Cor. 15:20)—The Firstfruits
Resurrection of Life (1 Cor. 15:23)—The Saints
Resurrection to Judgment (Rev. 20:13)—The Lost

485   The Intermediate State

The Present Abode of the Dead in Christ
"Unclothed" (2 Cor. 5:4)
"In Paradise" (Luke 23:43)
"With Christ" (Phil. 1:23)
"At Home with the Lord" (2 Cor. 5:8)

486   The Uncertainty of Life

Brief as a Flower (Job 14:2)
Swift as a Shuttle (Job 7:6)
Transient as a Shadow (Ps. 102:2)
Short as an Handbreadth (Ps. 39:5)

487 Notable Days in Man's History

Day of Birth (Job 14:1)
Day of Conversion (Luke 19:9)
Day of Death (Gen. 27:2)
Day of Resurrection (John 5:28)
Day of Judgment (Matt. 10:15)

488 The Believer's Hope

The Lord's Coming (1 Cor. 15:51)
To Be with Him (1 Thess. 4:17)
The Reunion with Friends (1 Thess. 4:17)
To See Him as He is (1 John 3:2)

489 Death Vanquished

Death Abolished (2 Tim. 1:10)—At the Cross
Death Swallowed Up (1 Cor. 15:54)—At the Advent
Death Destroyed (1 Cor. 15:26)—At the End

490 Eternity

(Isaiah 57:15)

The Eternal God (Deut. 33:27)—The Source
Eternal Salvation (Heb. 5:9)—The Supply
Eternal Glory (1 Peter 5:10)—The Saint's Prospect
Eternal Fire (Jude 7)—The Sinner's Doom

BLACKBOARD TOPICS

491   **Seedtime Lesson**

The **S**ower—The Lord Jesus (Matt. 13:3)
Seed—The Word of God (Luke 8:11)
Soils—Hearts of Sinners (Matt. 13:20-23)

492

LOST **S**heep (Luke 15:4)—Wandering
ilver (Luke 15:8)—Helpless
on (Luke 15:11)—Returning

493

BEHOLD I am Vile (Job 40:4)—Ruin
The Lamb (John 1:29)—Remedy
The Time (2 Cor. 6:2)—Reception

494

COME Invitation to the Weary (Matt. 11:28)
A Call to the Thirsty (John 7:37)
A Warning to the Careless (Isa. 1:18)
A Promise to the Sinful (2 Peter 3:10)

495   Jesus and the Children

(Luke 18:15, 16)

A *nxious* Mothers   **L** *ittle* Children
A *ngry* Disciples   **L** *oving* Savior

496   Brought and Blessed

(Mark 10:13-16)

B *rought* to **JESUS**
B *lessed* by **JESUS**

497   Trees

P *ulled Down* (1 Kings 5:6-9)—Conviction
lanted (Matt. 15:13)—Conversion
runed (John 15:2)—Education
lucked Up (Jude 12)—Exposure

498   Cords

C ords of Sin (Prov. 5:22)—Sinner's Bondage
ord of Scarlet (Josh. 2:18)—Savior's Blood
ords of Love (Hos. 11:4)—Saved One Drawn

499   "Unto Me"

		For
Turn	(Neh. 1:9)	Conversion
Come	(Matt. 11:28)	Reception
Look	(Isa. 45:22)	Healing
Pray	(Jer. 39:12)	Strength

UNTO **M**E

500   The Prodigal

D *eparture* (Luke 15:13)
issipation (Luke 15:13)
estitution (Luke 15:14)
egradation (Luke 15:5)
ecision (Luke 15:18)

INDEX

No.

A Birthday Carnival 332
A Fourfold Description of Man 50
A Grand Confession 465
A Harvest Address 479
A New Creation 272
A Pottery Address..........482
A Question and Its Answer..113
A Revival at Thessalonica...117
A Sevenfold Confession 220
A Threefold Cord of Love.... 23
A Threefold Cord of Salvation119
A Word to Harvesters.......478
Abram Justified 437
Abundant 136
Acceptance................. 69
Accepted and Acceptable 141
According to 325
Altars....................145
Always Ready 253
Aprons and Coats 434
At Caeserea Philippi 327
Atonement, The 450
Atonement, Advocacy, Advent 341
Attrition and Contrition 344

Balaam's Prayer 447
Behold 493
Believer's Hope.........86, 488
Believer's Sins Are 194
Best-known Bible Text, The .469
Bible Birds 236
Bible Plants 233
Bible Scenes 126
Blessed Is the Man.........180
Blood, The............387, 445
Blood and Hyssop, The......265
Blood and Water...........278
Blood and Wrath 166
Bond-servants 241
Bow and the Cloud, The 104
Brazen Serpent, The 452
Brought and Blessed 496
Brought Forth 401
Bundles 393

Cain and Abel.............435
Calls of Christ 156
Can We Be Sure of Salvation?433
Candles 383
Captive, Captain, and Cove-
    tous Servant, The 459
Children 216
Children of God 127
Christ and His Own........214
Christ Crucified 398
Christ Gave Himself 36
Christ, the Life 146
Christ, the Rock 128, 317
Christ, the Stone 264
Christ, the Word 370
Christ's Atonement 226
Christ's Lordship 254
Cities of Refuge, The 455
Cleansed, Clothed, Crowned .250
Cleansing 66, 213
Come 494
Common Proverbs..........293
Condemnation.............243
Contrasts 322, 323, 324
Conversion 205, 389
Cords 498
Cottage Meeting Address, A .476
Court Sermon, A 477
Crowns...................143

Daily Things in Early Church206
Darkness 135
Days.....................162
Death in Hebrews 2 343
Death to Life.............286
Death Vanquished 489
Debtors 339
Degrees of Faith 138
Difficulties Solved 281
Disciples 390
Divine Certainties 26
Divine Forgiveness 25
Divine Life 382
Divine Love..........173, 338

No.

Divine Wrath 400
Divinity of Christ, The 209
Does Death End All? 428
Does the Soul Sleep? 430
Doors 267
Doubts Dispelled 291

Ears .176
Earth, Heaven, and Hell 40
End, The 232
Eternal Life 386
Eternal Life in Three
    Aspects 105
Eternity 490
Everlasting Things 178, 399
Exceeding 130
Excepts 395
Excuses Explored 292
Eyes Opened 78

Faith 340
Faith and Works 58
Faith in Four Aspects 70
Far Off and Nigh 22
Fear Not 90
First and Last Words of Jesus 57
First Questions in Scripture .381
Five Baptisms 238
Five Cups 49
Five Looks of Jesus 55
Five Relationships to Christ .175
Five Yokes 41
Fools 88
Forgiveness 244
Forgiveness of Sins 108, 385
Found .163
Four "Alls" 45
Four "Cannots" 42
Four Confessions 193
Four Contrasts 121
Four Crowns 81
Four Foundation Facts 67
Four Gifts of God 158
Four Gospel "Mys" 15
Four Handwritings 65
Four Houses 191
Four Jehovah Titles 122
Four Legal Questions 352
Four Mighty Words 171
Four "One Things" 99
Four Present Blessings 28
Four Present Possessions 177
Four Reigns 334

No.

Four Seals 97
Four Steps in Sin 110
Four Straight Questions 31
Four Suppers 5
Four Thrones 60
Four Views of Christ's Work . 27
Fourfold Blessing 466
Fourfold Description of Man . 50
Fourfold Prayer 464
Fourfold View of the Sinner . 37
From Death to Life 286
From the Pit to the Crown . .288
Full Assurance 276
Fundamental Truths 228

Gate and Goal, The 483
Glorious Gospel, The 301
Glory of God, The 164
God and His People 72
God and the Sinner 118
God Is 258
God, Our Help 335
God's "Abundant " Things . . 13
God's Description of Man . . .161
God's "Musts" 259
God's Riches 249
God's Salvation 208
Gospel, The 227
Gospel A B C 96
Gospel Call, The 366
Gospel Feast, The 125
Gospel Hearers,
    Three Classes 29
Gospel Purity, ...346
Gospel Receivers 318
Gospel Rejectors 319
Gospel Signals 201
Grace 11
Grace and Judgment 261
Grace of God, The 33
Great Foundation Truths 235
Great Things 147
Great Transitions 359
Great White Throne, The . . . 19
Guilt, Grace, Glory 257

Hand of the Lord, The 53
Hands of Christ, The 61
Harvest Address, A 479
Harvest Past 480
Heart, The 230
Heaven and Hell Opened 219
His Name 56
How God Forgives Sinners . . . 14

No.

In Hell 140
Individual Conversations 92
Infinite Realities 199
Intermediate State, The 485
Is the Bible God's Word? 427
Is There a God? 429
Is There a Hell? 425
Is There Probation? 432
Isaiah's Conviction 481
Israel's Food 237
It Pleased God 123

Jehovah Revealed 361
Jesus and the Children 495
Jesus Christ, Faith's Object . . 247
Jesus Christ, the Lord 246
Jesus Christ, the Shepherd . . 245
Jesus, the Savior 182
Jonah's Voyage 462
Joseph and His Brethren 440
Joshua, the High Priest 460
Joy of God, The 84
Judgment 388
Justification in Four
    Aspects 373

Korah's Sin and Doom 453

Lamb, The 445
Lamps 234
Leper, The 448
Leper's Cleansing, The 449
Let Alone 268
Life From, in, and to Christ . 348
Life-giver and Judge 321
Life In the Spirit 64
Life, Light, Liberty 251
Life Look, The 294
Living Water 336
Look, Learn, Live 51
Looking Unto Jesus 129
Lord Jesus in Isaiah 53, The . 16
Lord Knoweth, The 134
Lord's Joy in Saving, The . . . 203
Lost Sheep, Silver, Son 492
Lost, The 330
Love Manifested, Com-
    mended, Bestowed 397
Love of God in Four Stages . . 379

Man, Christ Jesus, The 95
Manna, The 444

No.

Man's Guilt and God's
    Grace 468
Man's History 263
Man's Photograph 260
Man's Refusals of God's
    Grace 316
Man's Righteousness 169
Man's Way and Christ 277
Means 392
Mercy of God, The 157
Mightiest Work, The 470
Mighty One, The 155
Moriah 463

Naaman, the Leper 458
Name of Jesus, The 167
Names of Cities of Refuge . . . 456
New Birth, The 384
New Creation, A 272
No Difference 202
"No Mores" 12
No Neutrality 183
Noah and the Ark 436
Noah's Times and Testimony . 355
None 353
Notable Days 487
Nothings 82

"One Things," Four 99
Only One 312
Open-air Address, An 473
Opened and Closed 308
Opened Things 215
Our God 198
Our Names 256
Out of the Pit,
    Into the Service 17

Passover, The 445
Paul's Testimonies 360
Peace 4
Peace, False and True 225
Peace, Pattern, Power 310
Persuading 207
Popular Delusions 290
Pottery Address, A 482
Preacher and His Message . . 303
Preaching Christ 356
Precious Things 111
Prodigal, The 500
Profit and Loss 282

Questions . . . . 405 to 424

No.

Rahab's Faith 457
Ransom 328
Ready 179
Ready for Heaven or Hell . . .404
Rebekah's Call 439
Reconciliation 309
Red Sea, The 442
Redeemer and Redeemed 445
Redemption 239
Refuges 255
Refuges of Lies 285
Reserved and Kept 18
Rest .132
Rest, in Varied Aspects 299
Results of Preaching in Acts .337
Results of the Cross 302
"Resurgum" 484
Righteousness in Four
   Aspects 223
Righteousness of God, The . .218

Safe, Sure, Satisfied 262
Safety, Assurance, Peace 445
Salvation and Service 391
Salvation in Four Aspects . . . 10
Salvation Is of the Lord 368
Salvation of God, The . .107, 354
Salvation of the Lord 443
Salvation—Present 273
Sanctification 375
Sand and Rock 472
Satisfied 139
Saved 149
Saved and Being Saved 266
Saved, Sealed, Shown 403
Saved Sinner's Relation
   to Christ, The 137
Savior, The 211
Sea and its Wonders 471
Searching Questions 142
Seaside Sermons 471
Seedtime Lesson, A 491
Seeing Jesus 131
Sermon on Board Ship 475
Seven Eternal Things 68
Seven "I Ams" 101
Seven "I Wills" 441
Seven Things "Ready" 103
Sevenfold Virtue of the
   Blood 98
Shut In and Shut Out 331
Sin 240, 377
Sin, Sacrifice, Salvation 248

No.

Sinner's Destitution, The . . . 63
Sinner's Fear, Saint's
   Prospect 467
Sinner's Hope, The 85
Sinner's Three Stages 151
Six Foundation Truths 300
Slightly Healed 295
Smitten Rock, The 446
Sodom's Destruction 438
Some Bible Trees 32
Some Old Time Preachers . . .367
Son of God, The 195
Sons of Korah 454
Sower, Seed, Soil, The 280
Stone, The 369
Strong Man and Stronger . . .311
Stumbling-blocks Removed . .289
Sufferings of Christ, The 210
Swellings of Jordan, The 296
Swords 231

Tears .112
Things Exceeding 270
Things I Know 333
Things Poured Out 47
Things That Are Short 79
Things Which Are of God . . .351
Thou and Thy House 275
Three Appointments 46
Three "Beholdings" 6
Three "Beholds" of Christ . . .168
Three Blessings in
   John 10:9 20
Three Calls From Christ 106
Three Circles of Love 154
Three Classes in Hell 115
Three Classes of Gospel
   Hearers 150
Three Classes on Mars' Hill . 29
Three Comprehensive Words . 39
Three Conditions 197
Three Deaths 3
Three Divine Openings 54
Three Doors 52
Three "Excepts' 160
Three Fundamental Truths . .125
Three Golden Links 315
Three Gospel R's 252
Three Grand Realities 402
Three Great Life Truths 184
Three Great Questions 2
Three Invitations 153
Three Jehovah Titles 345

No.

Three "Musts" 38
Three Offices of Christ .165, 347
Three "Onlys" 1
Three "Past" Things 190
Three Periods 396
Three Personal Blessings....371
Three Personal Questions ...124
Three Present Blessings 89
Three Reigns, in Romans 5 .. 30
Three Representative Men....100
Three Salvation Truths 44
Three Solemn Facts 9
Three Stages in Grace 77
Three Stages of Christian
  Life 394
Three Stages of the Soul 93
Three Symbols of Christ's
  Work 186
Three Thousand Saved.....313
Three Typical Men.........196
Three "Unspeakable"
  Things.................. 24
Three "Withouts".......... 87
Three Words 74
Threefold Cord of Life 23
Threefold Crucifixion 48
Threefold Deliverance 91
Threefold Glory of Christ.... 73
Threefold Judgment 109
Threefold Justification 170
Threefold Rest 380
Threefold Salvation 43
Threefold Victory 192
Threefold View of Christ 224
Throne and Altar, The 229
Times and Seasons.........307
Tokens 187
Touch of Jesus, The 357
Trees 497
Triune God, The 34
True Tokens 271
Trumpets 80
Truth in Two Aspects.......181
Truth of God, The.......... 55
Two Divine Facts 120
Two Divine Realities 116
Two Great Facts 363
Two Great Works 62
Two Hard Things 189
Two Hours 305
Two Kinds of Fools 284
Two Masters 287
Two Meeting Places 212

No.

Two Night Visits 297
Two Pointed Questions......133
Two Prodigals 298
Two Roads, The............ 21
Two Seekers 314
Two Tremblers 320
Two Visages 185
Two "Whosoevers" 283
Twofold Cleansing 306
Twofold Redemption 376
Types ....434 to 463

Uncertainty of Life, The 486
Unconverted Professors 152
Unfruitful Seed............ 94
Universal Depravity 114
Unto Himself 71
"Unto Me"................499

Vessels 83
Voyage of Life, The 474

Warning, Winning,
  Watching 342
Watchman's Message, The ...304
Water of Life, The.......... 8
"We Know" 329
Weighed 269
What Christ Did and Does ..358
What Christ Is Able to Do ..102
What God Has Sent 349
What God Hath Made 159
What God Is, in Psalm 32 ... 75
What God Provides for
  Himself 372
What Grace Does 174
What Has Been Shed.......362
What the Gospel Ministers ..365
What the Word Does 59
Whole World, The..........350
Whom God Justifies........279
Whom Jesus Saves 217
Will All Men Be Saved? 431
Windows 144
Windows of Heaven 242
Wings....................172
Winter Scenes............481
With all the Heart 200
Witnesses to Christ 76
Word Is Able, The..........188
Word of God and Believers ..222
Word, The, and Unconverted .221
Word to Harvesters, A 478

No.

No.

Work of Christ, The 374

Works....................148

Work of God in the Soul 364

Wrath of God, The 374

Work of Righteousness, The ..274

Work of the Spirit 326, 378

Year of Jubilee, The 451

Other Sermon Outline Titles:

Briggs, S.R. and Elliot, J.H.
  600 BIBLE GEMS AND OUTLINES

Jabez Burns Sermon Outline Series
  149 SERMON OUTLINES
  151 SERMON OUTLINES
  199 SERMON OUTLINES
  200 SERMON OUTLINES
  201 SERMON OUTLINES
  91 SERMON OUTLINES ON TYPES AND METAPHORS

Marsh, F.E.
  500 BIBLE STUDY OUTLINES
  1000 BIBLE STUDY OUTLINES
  ILLUSTRATED BIBLE STUDY OUTLINES

John Ritchie Sermon Outline Series
  500 SERMON OUTLINES ON BASIC BIBLE TRUTHS
  500 CHILDREN'S SERMON OUTLINES
  500 EVANGELISTIC SERMON OUTLINES
  500 GOSPEL ILLUSTRATIONS
  500 GOSPEL SERMON OUTLINES
  500 SERMON OUTLINES ON THE CHRISTIAN LIFE

Easy-to-Use Sermon Outline Series
Edited by Charles R. Wood
  EVANGELISTIC SERMON OUTLINES
  REVIVAL SERMON OUTLINES
  SERMON OUTLINES FOR FUNERAL SERVICES
  SERMON OUTLINES FOR SPECIAL DAYS AND OCCASIONS
  SERMON OUTLINES FOR TEENS
  SERMON OUTLINES FROM PROVERBS
  SERMON OUTLINES FROM THE SERMON ON THE MOUNT
  SERMON OUTLINES ON THE PSALMS